American English File

Workbook 1

Clive Oxenden
Christina Latham-Koenig
Paul Seligson

with Jane Hudson

OXFORD
UNIVERSITY PRESS

Paul Seligson and Clive Oxenden are the original co-authors of *English File 1* (pub. 1996) and *English File 2* (pub. 1997).

UNIVERSITY PRESS

198 Madison Avenue
New York, NY 10016 USA

Great Clarendon Street, Oxford OX2 6DP UK

Oxford University Press is a department of the University of Oxford. It furthers the University's objective of excellence in research, scholarship, and education by publishing worldwide in

Oxford New York

Auckland Cape Town Dar es Salaam Hong Kong Karachi Kuala Lumpur Madrid Melbourne Mexico City Nairobi New Delhi Shanghai Taipei Toronto

With offices in

Argentina Austria Brazil Chile Czech Republic France Greece Guatemala Hungary Italy Japan Poland Portugal Singapore South Korea Switzerland Thailand Turkey Ukraine Vietnam

OXFORD and OXFORD ENGLISH are registered trademarks of Oxford University Press.

Editorial Director: Sally Yagan
Publisher: Laura Pearson
Managing Editor: Anna Teevan
Project Editor: Maria A. Dalsenter
Design Director: Robert Carangelo
Project Leader: Bridget McGoldrick
Manufacturing Manager: Shanta Persaud
Manufacturing Controller: Eve Wong

ISBN: 978 0 19 477418 5 WORKBOOK WITH MULTI-ROM (PACK)
ISBN: 978 0 19 477419 2 WORKBOOK (PACK COMPONENT)
ISBN: 978 0 19 477420 8 MULTI-ROM (PACK COMPONENT)

Printed in China

11

Acknowledgments

Design by: Amanda Hockin
Cover design by: Jaclyn Smith

The authors would like to thank all those at Oxford University Press who have contributed their skills and ideas to producing this course.

And very special thanks from Clive to Maria Angeles and from Christina to Cristina for all their help and encouragement. Christina would also like to thank her children Joaquin, Marco, and Krysia for their constant inspiration.

The publisher and authors are grateful to those who have given permission to reproduce the following extracts and adaptations of copyright material: p. 23 "Bond girl formula revealed" from www.ananova.com. Reproduced by permission; p. 34 Information from www.centerparcs.co.uk. Reproduced by permission; p. 45 "Japanese businessman gets on Edinburgh party bus instead of airport bus" from www.ananova.com. Reproduced by permission; p. 52 Information from www.laperlalivingrentals.com. Reproduced by permission; p. 63 "20 dream holidays for the 21st Century" by Jill Crawshaw, *The Observer* 26th January 2003 © Jill Crawshaw. Reproduced by permission; p. 74 "Mountaintop proposal backfires when couple drop ring" from www.ananova.com. Reproduced by permission; p. 79 *J.K. Rowling biography* by Betty Jimenez © 2001 by PageWise, Inc. Used with permission.

The publisher would like to thank the following for their permission to reproduce photographs: Age Fotostock p. 57 (Bartomeu Amengual); Alamy pp. 16 (David/Rubber Ball, Dino/Photofusion), 48 (memory card/David J. Green, Mexico), 62 (Shout), 67 (Fiat/Marc Zakian), 68 (Brand X Pictures), 72 (wine/Cephas Picture Library); Associated Press pp. 29 (Saurabh Das), 79 (Louis M Lanzano); Black Horse Hotel p. 21; Brand X p. 10 (coins/Robertstock); Center Parcs p. 34; Corbis Images pp. 41 (Hendrix, Ghandi /Hulton Deutsch Collection, Gable/Bettman), 43 (Wall Street/Bettman, early television/Schenectady Museum); Getty Images pp. 6 (Cosmo Condina), 8 (Jon Feingersh), 9 (Neil Beckermann), 16 (Aisha/Chabruken, William), 18 (man/Tim McGuire, Caucasian woman/Ryan Mcvay, Asian woman/Howard Kingsnorth), 25 (woman at home/Antony Nagelmann, women at restaurant/Michael Goldman), 28 (Ross Anania), 30 (coffee machine), 33 (David Madison), 35 (friends/Betsie Van der Meer, couple/Romilly Lockyer), 41 (Frida Kahlo/Hulton Archive), 50 (Dom.Doc), 55 (Julie Toy), 72 (water skiing/Alan Becker, wallpaper/Diana Koenigsberg); La Perla Living Rentals p. 52; Index Stock p. 39 (Tokyo/Nordic Photos); Inmagine pp. 44 (Corbis), 60 (violin/Photodisc); Photo Edit Inc. p. 10 (magazine/Michael Newman); Press Association pp. 54 (Toby Melville), 67 (Ferrari); Randolph Hotel p. 21; Rex Features pp. 23 (Everett Collection), 38 (Tony Eyles), 43 (George Harrison/Harry Goodwin), 69 (Paul Cooper); Terry Taylor Studio p. 48 (mug); The Image Works p. 10 (stamps/Rommel Pecson); Westwood Country Hotel p. 21

Illustrations by: Nick Baker p. 24 (woman); Stephen Conlin p. 56; Paul Daviz pp. 23, 53 (park); Mark Duffin pp. 7, 12 (signs), 16, 19, 21, 24 (clocks), 25, 27, 30 (coffee, cappuccino, cookies, brownie), 39 (clothes), 48 (photos, T-shirts, batteries), 49, 51 (seafront), 57, 59, 60 (watch, wallet, vase, bicycle, boots), 61, 63; Martha Gavin pp. 12 (restaurant), 36, 39 (couple), 66, 74, 75; Ginna Magee pp. 7 (choose), 15, 61 (apple juice, soda); Ellis Nadler pronunciation symbols; Nigel Paige pp. 11, 31, 46, 47, 70; Colin Shelbourn pp. 17, 22, 31 (crossword cues), 40, 42, 53 (grandma), 65, 73; Andy Smith p. 4 (taxi), 64; Kath Walker pp. 4, 5, 13, 14, 26, 32, 37, 51 (ghost), 58 (couple), 60 (interviews), 71, 76, 77

Commissioned photography by: Mark Mason pp. 10 (comb, lipstick, pen, tissues, wallet, pencil, glasses, watch, keys), 58

Contents

My name's Bond. James Bond.
Ian Fleming, British writer

Nice to meet you

1 SAYING HELLO

Complete the dialogues.

1 **A** Hi, Karen. *This* is James.
B Hello, James. ______ to ______ you.

2 **A** Hi, I'm Marco. ______'s your ______?
B Isabella.
A ______?
B Isabella!

3 **A** Hi, Kenji. ______ are you?
B I'm fine, thanks. And ______?
A I'm OK, thank you.

4 **A** ______ evening. What's your name?
B ______ ______'s Walter Harris.
A You're in room 12.

2 GRAMMAR verb *be* [+], pronouns

a Complete the first column with the words in the box. Then write the contractions.

she are they is I are is are

Full form	Contractions
I am	*I'm*
you ______	______
he ______	______
______ is	______
it ______	______
we ______	______
you ______	______
______ are	______

b Complete the sentences. Use contractions.

1 *I'm* 4.

2 ______ tourists.

3 ______ in room 4.

4 ______ Wednesday.

5 ______ in a taxi.

6 ______ a teacher.

7 ______ in room 603.

8 Hello. ______ in my class.

Study Link **Student Book p.122** *Grammar Bank 1A*

3 PRONUNCIATION vowel sounds, word stress

a Write the words in the chart.

meet	you	fine	two	six	man
eight	three	nice	in	thank	wait

ɪ fish	i tree	æ cat	u boot	eɪ train	aɪ bike
six					

b Underline the stressed syllable in these words.

1 coffee
2 afternoon
3 eighteen
4 thirteen
5 evening
6 good–bye
7 e-mail
8 Internet
9 computer
10 hotel

c Practice saying the words in **a** and **b**.

4 VOCABULARY numbers 1–20

Continue the series.

1 five, six, seven, *eight*, *nine*, *ten*.
2 six, eight, ten, ______, ______, ______.
3 twenty, nineteen, ______, ______, ______.
4 five, seven, nine, ______, ______, ______.
5 one, four, seven, ______, ______, ______.

Study Link **Student Book p.140** *Vocabulary Bank*

5 SAYING GOOD–BYE

a Complete the words with *a*, *e*, *i*, *o*, or *u*.

b Put the letters in order to make days of the week.

1 ARSAYDUT *Saturday*
2 NYAUDS ______
3 HRDYTUSA ______
4 ODNYMA ______
5 DFARYI ______
6 DSYEEAWND ______
7 EUASDTY ______

More Words to Learn

Write translations and try to remember the words.

Word	Pronunciation	Translation
room *noun*	/rʊm/ or /rum/	
word *noun*	/wərd/	
morning *noun*	/ˈmɔrnɪŋ/	
afternoon *noun*	/æftərˈnun/	
evening *noun*	/ˈivnɪŋ/	
good *adjective*	/gʊd/	
important *adjective*	/ɪmˈpɔrtnt/	
help *verb*	/hɛlp/	
try *verb*	/traɪ/	
check *verb*	/tʃɛk/	

Study idea

To remember new words, you need to test your memory.

1 Cover the **Translation** column and look at the words in English. Say them in your language.
2 Cover the **Word** column and look at the translation. Say the words in English.

QUESTION TIME

Can you answer these questions?

1 What's your name?
2 How are you?
3 What day is it today?
4 Is it Monday today?
5 Are you a teacher?

Study Link **MultiROM**

To be or not to be, that is the question.
William Shakespeare, English playwright

I'm not American, I'm Canadian!

1 VOCABULARY countries and nationalities

Complete with a country or a nationality.

1 Alice is from the United States. She's *American*.
2 Duncan is Scottish. He's from *Scotland*.
3 Jun is from China. He's ____________.
4 My friends are Mexican. They're from ____________.
5 Sandra is from Argentina. She's ____________.
6 Toyota cars are Japanese. They're from ____________.
7 Spaghetti is from Italy. It's ____________.
8 We're French. We're from ____________.
9 She's from Korea. She's ____________.
10 They're Spanish. They're from ____________.

Study Link **Student Book p.141** *Vocabulary Bank*

2 GRAMMAR verb *be* [–] and [?]

a Correct the sentences.

1 Venice is in Greece. (Italy)
Venice isn't in Greece. It's in Italy.
2 Sean Connery is Irish. (Scottish)
____________.
3 I'm American. (British)
____________.
4 Osaka and Kyoto are in China. (Japan)
____________.
5 We're in room 104. (room 105)
____________.
6 Tacos are from Italy. (Mexico)
____________.
7 You're Canadian. (French)
____________.
8 Cameron Diaz is Spanish. (American)
____________.

b Order the words to make questions.

1 your / 's / name / What
What's your name?
2 she / Where / 's / from
____________?
3 United / from / they / States / the / Are
____________?
4 seven / room / we / in / Are
____________?
5 vacation / you / Are / on
____________?
6 from / he / Japan / Is
____________?

c Match these answers to the questions in **b**.

a Yes, he is. [6]
b No, I'm not. [ ]
c She's from Thailand. [ ]
d No, we aren't. [ ]
e Yes, they are. [ ]
f Andrew. [ ]

Study Link **Student Book p.122** *Grammar Bank 1B*

3 PRONUNCIATION vowel sounds

a Write the words in the chart.

~~Argentina~~ twenty **air**port n**o**t
h**o**tel wh**ere** **are** c**o**py Japan
Mexic**o** W**e**dnesday hundr**e**d

ɑr car	ɑ clock	ə computer	ɛ egg	oʊ phone	ɛr chair
Argentina	______	______	______	______	______
______	______	______	______	______	______

b Underline the stressed syllable in these words.

1 Spanish
2 Japan
3 Japanese
4 Germany
5 China
6 Brazil
7 Portuguese
8 Italy
9 Italian
10 American

c Practice saying the words in **a** and **b**.

4 VOCABULARY numbers 20–1,000

a Write the numbers in words.

1 27 *twenty-seven*
2 33 ______
3 40 ______
4 56 ______
5 77 ______
6 85 ______
7 100 ______
8 240 ______
9 677 ______
10 1,000 ______

b Cover the words. Practice saying the numbers.

Study Link **Student Book p.140** *Vocabulary Bank*

5 INSTRUCTIONS

a Match the words and pictures.

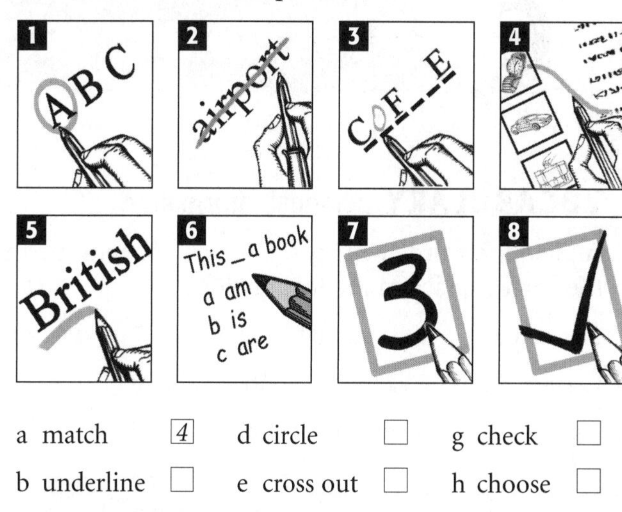

a match [4]
b underline ☐
c complete ☐
d circle ☐
e cross out ☐
f number ☐
g check ☐
h choose ☐

b Cover the words. Look at the pictures and try to remember the words.

More Words to Learn

Write translations and try to remember the words.

Word	Pronunciation	Translation
people *noun*	/ˈpipl/	
things *noun*	/θɪŋz/	
quiz *noun*	/kwɪz/	
difference *noun*	/ˈdɪfrəns/	
vacation *noun*	/veɪˈkeɪʃn/	
business *noun*	/ˈbɪznəs/	
music *noun*	/ˈmyuzɪk/	
city *noun*	/ˈsɪti/	
delicious *adjective*	/dɪˈlɪʃəs/	
again *adverb*	/əˈgɛn/	

QUESTION TIME

Can you answer these questions?

1 What nationality are you?
2 Where are you from?
3 What's the language in your country?
4 What's your phone number?
5 Are you on vacation?

Study Link **MultiROM**

Forgive your enemies, but never forget their names.
John F. Kennedy, former American president

His name, her name

1 VOCABULARY personal information

Complete the words with *a*, *e*, *i*, *o*, or *u*. Then write them in the correct place in the form below.

1 z*i*p c*o*d*e* 4 _-m__l _ddr_ss 7 _ddr_ss
2 f_rst n_m_ 5 c_ty / c__ntry 8 l_st n_m_
3 _g_ 6 ph_n_ n_mb_r 9 st_d_nt

The Toronto School

application form

1	________	Alessandra
2	________	Bellucci
3	________	Porto Alegre / Brazil
4	________	No
5	________	30
6	________	Rua Minerva, 6
7	*zip code*	90110
8	________	bellucci@hitmail.com
9	________	555–3821

2 PRONUNCIATION the alphabet

a Circle the letter with a different vowel sound.

eɪ train	i tree	u boot	ɛ egg	aɪ bike
H	C	Q	F	E
J	P	U	A	I
(G)	S	O	M	Y

b Practice saying the letters.

3 GRAMMAR possessive adjectives

a Complete the chart.

Subject pronoun	Possessive adjective
I	
	your
he	
	her
	its
we	
you	
	their

b Complete the sentences with a possessive adjective.

1 *Her* name's Susana.
2 ________ name's Michael.
3 We're students. ________ teacher's name's Richard.
4 I'm French. ________ family is from Lyon.
5 It's an Italian restaurant. ________ name is Luigi's.
6 **A** What's ________ phone number?
B My cell phone number?
7 They're Mexican. ________ last name's Gómez.

c Order the words to make questions.

1 first / her / What's / name
What's her first name? Maria.
2 teacher / Where / from / your / 's
________________? The US.
3 he / student / Is / a
________________? No, he isn't.
4 you / old / How / are
________________? I'm 34.
5 name / spell / do / How / you / your / last
________________? L-O-W-R-Y.

Study Link **Student Book p.122** *Grammar Bank 1C*

4 PRONUNCIATION /ər/ and /aʊ/

a Circle the word with a different vowel sound.

ər	b**ir**d	th**ir**ty the**ir** G**er**man Th**ur**sday
aʊ	**ow**l	th**ou**sand h**ow** y**ou** **ou**r

b Underline the stressed syllable in these words.

1 student 4 number

2 address 5 Canada

3 e-mail 6 Australia

c Practice saying the words in **a** and **b**.

5 READING

a Read the interview and write the questions in the correct space.

Are you married?	What's her name?
~~What's your name?~~	How old are you?
Where are you from?	Where's the language school?

b Look at the highlighted words. What do you think they mean? Check your dictionary.

Interview with
a language teacher

1 *What's your name?*

My name's Thomas, but people call me Tom.

2 ______________________________?

I'm from Sheffield in the north of England, but now I live in Lisbon, in Portugal. I'm an English teacher. I work at a language school.

3 ______________________________?

Yes, I am. My wife is Portuguese.

4 ______________________________?

Her name's Juliana. We have two children. Laura is 5, and Victor is 2. They speak English and Portuguese.

5 ______________________________?

I'm 35.

6 ______________________________?

It's in the center of Lisbon. It's a small school with about 200 students.

More Words to Learn

Write translations and try to remember the words.

Word	Pronunciation	Translation
Australia *noun*	/ɔ'streɪlyə/	
Canada *noun*	/'kænədə/	
form *noun*	/fɔrm/	
letter (A, B, C…) *noun*	/'lɛtər/	
international *adjective*	/ɪntər'næʃənl/	
different *adjective*	/'dɪfrənt/	
famous *adjective*	/'feɪməs/	
think *verb*	/θɪŋk/	
about *adverb*	/ə'baʊt/	
every *adjective*	/'ɛvri/	

QUESTION TIME

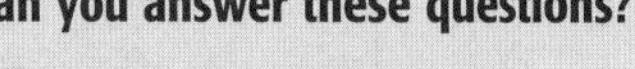

Can you answer these questions?

1 What's your first name?

2 What's your last name?

3 Are you a student?

4 How old are you?

5 What's your address?

Study Link MultiROM

Mr. Watson, come here.
Alexander Graham Bell, inventor, to his assistant (the first telephone conversation)

Turn off your cell phones!

1 VOCABULARY common objects

Complete the crossword.

Study Link Student Book p.142 *Vocabulary Bank*

2 PRONUNCIATION vowel sounds

a Write the words in the chart.

good coins here Europe we're ~~four~~ board country euro hundred book enjoy

ɔr horse	ʊ bull	ʌ up	ɔɪ boy	ɪr ear	ʊr tourist
four					

b Practice saying the words.

3 GRAMMAR *a / an*, plurals, *this / that / these / those*

a Write *It's + a/an* or *They're.*

1 *It's an* address book.
2 *They're* tissues.
3 ______ newspaper.
4 ______ ID card.
5 ______ sunglasses.
6 ______ umbrella.
7 ______ coins.
8 ______ change purse.

b Write each word in its plural form in the correct column.

~~coin~~ match sandwich family wallet dictionary pen ~~watch~~ pencil ~~country~~ city address

-s	-es	-ies
coins	*watches*	*countries*

c Complete the sentences with *this*, *that*, *these*, or *those*.

1 *That* picture's nice!

2 ____________ are my friends, Mom.

3 ____________ man's my English teacher!

4 I think ____________ people are tourists.

5 What's ____________? It's a newspaper.

Study Link **Student Book p.122** *Grammar Bank 1D*

4 CLASSROOM LANGUAGE

a Complete the sentences.

1 *Close* the door.
2 L____________ to the teacher.
3 O____________ your books.
4 W____________ in pairs.
5 Don't w____________.
6 T____________ off your cell phone.
7 L____________ at the board.
8 Don't s____________ Spanish.

b Order the words to make sentences.

1 don't / I / know
I don't know.
2 do / How / it / you / spell
____________________________________?
3 don't / I / understand
____________________________________.
4 you / it / Can / please / repeat
____________________________________?
5 in / English / How / you / say / do / *vacaciones*
____________________________________?
6 remember / I / don't
____________________________________.

More Words to Learn

Write translations and try to remember the words.

Word	Pronunciation	Translation
classroom *noun*	/ˈklæsrum/	
eyes *noun*	/aɪz/	
instructions *noun*	/ɪnˈstrʌkʃnz/	
pocket *noun*	/ˈpɑkət/	
happy *adjective*	/ˈhæpi/	
worry *verb*	/ˈwəri/	
point *verb*	/pɔɪnt/	
guess *verb*	/gɛs/	
see *verb*	/si/	
please *interjection*	/pliz/	

QUESTION TIME

Can you answer these questions?

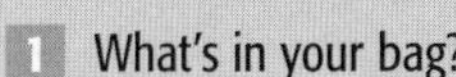

1 What's in your bag?
2 How do you spell *coffee*?
3 Where's the stress in *coffee*?
4 Is this your book?
5 How do you say *door* in your language?

Study Link **MultiROM**

On a plane

1 VOCABULARY drinks

Order the letters. What are the drinks?

1 KILM *milk*
2 FECOFE ______
3 RETWA ______
4 AET ______
5 ANROEG CIJEU ______
6 ODAS ______

2 ASKING FOR A DRINK

Complete the conversations. Write one word in each blank.

A Would you like a drink, sir?
B Yes, a mineral 1 *water*, please.
A Ice and lemon?
B 2 J______ lemon.

A Tea or coffee?
B Tea, 3 p______.
A Milk?
B 4 Y______, please.
A Sugar?
B No, 5 t______.

3 SOCIAL ENGLISH

Complete the dialogue with these words.

Can Let's ~~Nice~~ OK Welcome

A Hello. Are you Jack Horton?
B Yes. Are you Min?
A Yes, I am. 1 *Nice* to meet you.
B You too. 2______ to Korea. 3______ I help you with your bags?
A No. It's 4______, thanks.
B My car's in the parking lot. Would you like a coffee first?
A No, thanks. I'm fine.
B All right. 5______ go.

4 READING

a Match the words and pictures.

phones baggage claim taxis ~~restrooms~~ departures parking lot bar arrivals carts

1 *restrooms* 2 ______ 3 ______
4 ______ 5 ______ 6 ______
7 ______ 8 ______ 9 ______

b Read the dialogues. Where are they? Write the number from **a**.

1 **A** Two sodas, please.
B Ice and lemon? [7]

2 **A** Good morning. Where to?
B Downtown, please.
A OK, let's go. [ ]

3 **A** Good–bye, Cathy. Have a good trip!
B Bye, Paul. See you soon. [ ]

4 **A** Look! Is that your bag?
B No, my bag's black. Ah, there it is! [ ]

5 **A** Hi, it's me.
B Where are you?
A I'm at the airport. [ ]

c Underline five words or phrases you don't know. Use your dictionary to look up their meaning and pronunciation.

All I know is what I read in the papers.
Will Rogers, American comedian

Cappuccino and fries

1 VOCABULARY verb phrases

Complete the verb phrases.

French ~~dinner~~ TV in an apartment
a car a magazine to the movies glasses

1 cook *dinner*
2 drive ______
3 speak ______
4 read ______
5 watch ______
6 wear ______
7 live ______
8 go ______

Study Link **Student Book p.143** *Vocabulary Bank*

2 VOCABULARY irregular plurals

a Complete the chart.

Singular	Plural
man	
	children
person	
	women

b Complete the sentences with a word from the chart in a.

1 Her mother is a very nice *person*.
2 I have two ______. My first ______ is six years old.
3 Many American ______ drink coffee.
4 Don't go into that restroom, David! It's for ______, not ______.

3 GRAMMAR simple present + and −

a Circle the correct answer.

1 A lot of American people (**go**) / **goes** to the movies.
2 They **don't smoke** / **doesn't smoke** in coffeehouses.
3 We **read** / **reads** the newspaper on the train.
4 They **doesn't like** / **don't like** children in restaurants.
5 You **lives** / **live** in a house with a yard.
6 My father **don't cook** / **doesn't cook**.
7 In the US, cars **stop** / **stops** at crosswalks.
8 The women **do** / **does** the housework in my family.
9 My mother **watch** / **watches** a lot of TV.
10 Your children **eat** / **eats** a lot of French fries.

b Look at the chart and complete the **You** column.

	Tom	Susan	You
drink tea	✗	✓	
eat pasta	✓	✗	
watch TV in the evening	✓	✓	
play the piano	✗	✗	

Now complete the sentences.

1 Tom *eats* pasta.
2 Tom ______ tea.
3 Susan and Tom ______ TV in the evening.
4 I ______ the piano.
5 Susan ______ tea.
6 I ______ television in the evening.
7 Tom and Susan ______ the piano.
8 I ______ pasta.
9 I ______ tea.
10 Susan ______ pasta.

c Complete the sentences.

1 I _don't smoke_ (not / smoke).

2 My mother __________ (study) English.

3 They __________ (not / go) to school.

4 She __________ (have) two children.

5 The restaurant __________ (close) at 11:00.

6 We __________ (not / have) a yard.

7 Her father __________ (not / work).

Study Link **Student Book p.124** *Grammar Bank 2A*

4 PRONUNCIATION consonant sounds, -s

a Write the words in the chart.

smoke **w**ork ~~**h**ave~~ doe**s** typica**l** stan**d**
ha**s** T**V** **d**rive **l**ike cook**s** **wh**en

v **v**ase	d **d**og	s **s**nake	z **z**ebra	l **l**eg	w **w**itch
have	______	______	______	______	______
______	______	______	______	______	______

b Circle the word which ends in /ɪz/.

1 lives	works	(dances)
2 drinks	likes	washes
3 drives	finishes	plays
4 watches	cooks	speaks
5 reads	stops	kisses
6 catches	eats	goes

c Practice saying the words in **a** and **b**.

More Words to Learn

Write translations and try to remember the words.

Word	Pronunciation	Translation
popular *adjective*	/'pɑpyələr/	
incredible *adjective*	/ɪn'krɛdəbl/	
typical *adjective*	/'tɪpɪkl/	
fantastic *adjective*	/fæn'tæstɪk/	
terrible *adjective*	/'tɛrəbl/	
just (= only) *adverb*	/dʒʌst/	
everywhere *adverb*	/'ɛvriwɛr/	
really *adverb*	/'rili/	
too *adverb*	/tu/	
a lot of *quantifier*	/eɪ lɑt əv/	
many *quantifier*	/'mɛni/	

Study idea

1 Use your dictionary to find the meaning, the grammar, and the pronunciation of new words.

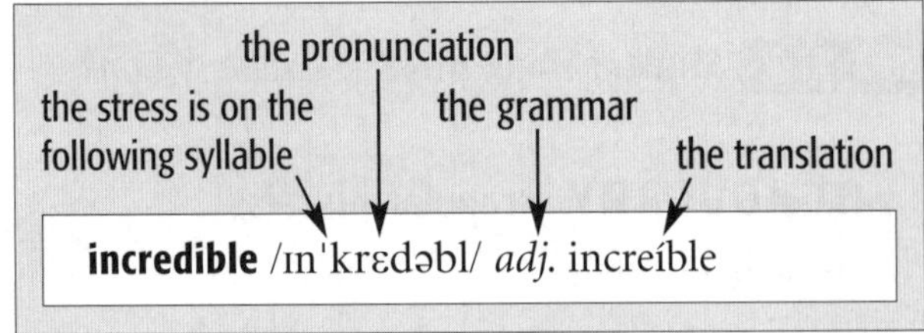

2 Look at the **Pronunciation** column above. Say the words two or three times.

Popular … popular … popular.

QUESTION TIME

Can you answer these questions?

1 Do you smoke?

2 Do you live in an apartment?

3 Do you like soccer?

4 Do you read a newspaper every day?

5 Do you wear glasses?

Study Link **MultiROM**

Study Link www.oup.com/elt/americanenglishfile/1

It's relaxing to go out with my ex-wife because she already knows I'm an idiot.
Warren Thomas, American writer

When Natasha meets Darren...

1 GRAMMAR simple present [?]

a Complete the questions with *Do* or *Does.*

1. ___*Do*___ you live in a house?
2. ________ your parents work in an office?
3. ________ your sister have a dog?
4. ________ you speak Japanese?
5. ________ your mother drive a BMW?
6. ________ James play the piano?
7. ________ your father smoke?
8. ________ they have lunch at home?
9. ________ Ann do homework on the weekend?
10. ________ you go on vacation every year?

b Order the words to make questions.

1. with / Do / live / your / you /mother
   Do you live with your mother?
2. Where / have / does / lunch / Kate
   ______________________________?
3. go / do / to / movies / When / you / the
   ______________________________?
4. listen / you / in / the / the / Do / to / radio / morning
   ______________________________?
5. they / Where / soccer / do / play
   ______________________________?
6. she / Does / French / study
   ______________________________?
7. brother / the / work / his / Does / hotel / in /
   ______________________________?
8. friends / When / do / play / your / tennis
   ______________________________?
9. have / do / When / lunch / you
   ______________________________?
10. work / in / office / Do / an / they
   ______________________________?

c Dong and Rachel are new friends. They go out for coffee. Complete the questions.

R So, Dong, [1] ___*where do you live*___?
D In Seoul. In a small house.
R [2] ______________ with your parents?
D Yes, and my sister. What about you?
[3] ______________ any brothers and sisters?
R I have a brother. He's 19.
D [4] ______________ work?
R No, he's a student.
D What about you? [5] ______________ work?
R In a store downtown.
D [6] ______________ your job?
R Yes, I like it a lot.

Study Link Student Book p.124 *Grammar Bank 2B*

2 PRONUNCIATION consonant sounds

a Circle the word with a different sound.

k	**k**ey	**c**ountry **c**ook (center) **c**offee
g	**g**irl	**g**et **G**ermany **g**olf **g**o
ʃ	**sh**ower	**sh**e fi**sh** gla**ss**es Ru**ss**ia

b Practice saying the words.

3 VOCABULARY common verb phrases

Who's the best boyfriend for Aisha?

Aisha is 29. She wants to find a boyfriend. She [1] *lives* in Montreal, and she [2] ____________ in a hospital. She [3] ____________ to New York on vacation. She [4] ____________ TV, but she [5] ____________ to classical music. She [6] ____________ Italian food in her kitchen at home.

William is 42. He [7] ____________ the newspaper and watches TV on weekends. He works in an office and [8] ____________ a BMW. He lives in a big house and [9] ____________ the piano.

David is 30. He [10] ____________ the electric guitar. He [11] ____________ fast food, but he [12] ____________ soda. He [13] ____________ soccer all weekend in the park.

Dino is 26. He's Italian, but he [14] ____________ in Canada. He [15] ____________ medicine. He [16] ____________ four languages. He [17] ____________ to the movies on Saturdays. He [18] ____________ going to restaurants.

a Complete the sentences with a verb in the correct form.

read go (x2) study drive work not watch
play (x3) not eat live (x2) listen speak
cook not like drink

b Read the text again. Who would be the best boyfriend for Aisha – William, David, or Dino?

4 INSTRUCTIONS

a Match the words and pictures.

1 

2 

3 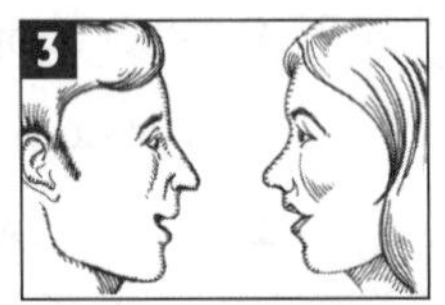

4 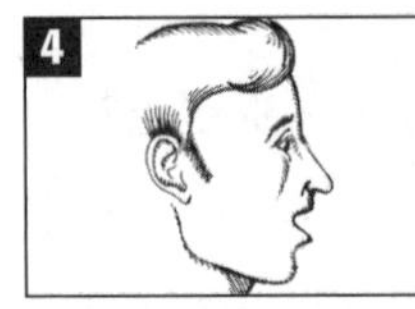

5 

6 

7 

8 

a ask [1]	d cover the text [ ]	g think [ ]
b answer [ ]	e test a partner [ ]	h copy [ ]
c say [ ]	f role–play [ ]	

b Cover the words. Look at the pictures and try to remember the words.

More Words to Learn

Write translations and try to remember the words.

Word	Pronunciation	Translation
friends *noun*	/frɛndz/	
boyfriend *noun*	/ˈbɔɪfrɛnd/	
girlfriend *noun*	/ˈgərlfrɛnd/	
glass (of water) *noun*	/glæs/	
supermarket *noun*	/ˈsupərmɑrkət/	
north, south, east, west *nouns*	/nɔrθ/ /saʊθ/ /ist/ /wɛst/	
cook *verb*	/kʊk/	
late *adjective*	/leɪt/	
Let's meet…	/lɛts mit/	

QUESTION TIME

Can you answer these questions?

1 Where do you live?
2 What languages do you speak?
3 Do you have a car?
4 What sports do you play?
5 What food do you like?

Study Link **MultiROM**

Study Link www.oup.com/elt/americanenglishfile/1

Every child is an artist. The problem is how to remain an artist when he grows up.

Pablo Picasso, Spanish painter

2C An artist and a musician

1 VOCABULARY jobs

a Complete the crossword.

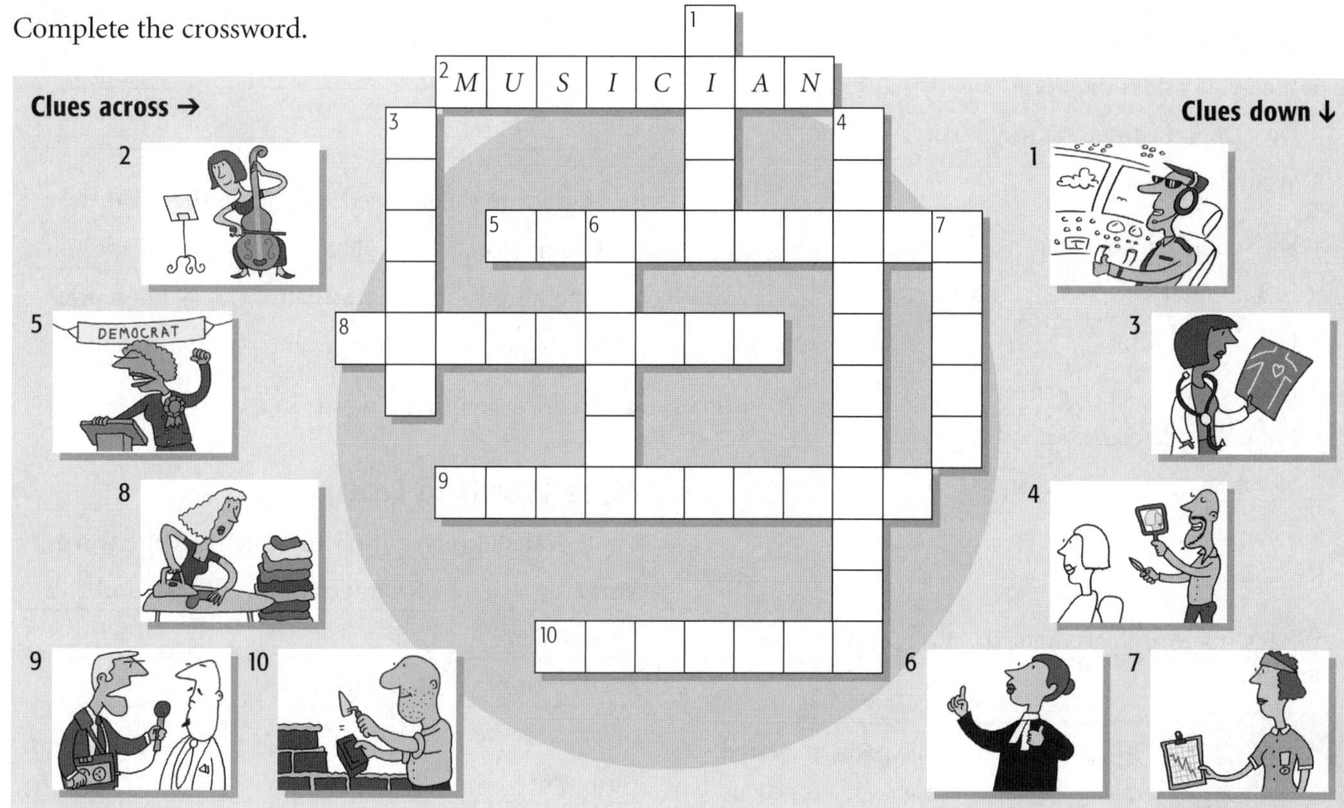

b Write *er* or *or*.

1 soccer play*er* 3 act__ 5 doct__

2 manag__ 4 wait__ 6 police offic__

c Complete the sentences with these words.

just lonely ~~draw~~ every day in a hurry stressful vacation

1 Artists are people who *draw* and paint pictures.

2 I don't have breakfast when I'm ________.

3 David has 28 days of ________ every year.

4 My father drinks four cups of coffee ________.

5 My boyfriend has a very ________ job.

6 People who work at home are sometimes ________.

7 I ________ have a sandwich for lunch.

d Complete the sentences with these words.

at (2x) with (2x) in (3x) of for (2x)

1 My sister works *for* the government.

2 I work ______ three other people.

3 I'm 16, and I'm ______ school.

4 They work ______ a hospital.

5 Maria works ______ an office.

6 Her brother works ______ a newspaper.

7 Jack works ______ home.

8 My boyfriend studies economics ______ college.

9 Maria earns a lot ______ money.

10 Do you work ______ a computer?

Study Link **Student Book p.144** *Vocabulary Bank*

2 GRAMMAR *a* / *an* + jobs

a Circle the correct form. Then complete the answers with *a*, *an*, or –. Then match the questions and answers.

1 What **do** / **does** he do? [c]
2 What **do** / **does** they do? [ ]
3 **Is** / **Does** she a housewife? [ ]
4 What **do** / **does** you do? [ ]
5 **Is** / **Are** they politicians? [ ]
6 Where **do** / **does** she work? [ ]
7 **Do** / **Does** they study at a university? [ ]
8 What **does** / **do** she do? [ ]

a She's ___*a*___ hairdresser.
b In a hospital – she's ______ nurse.
c He's ______ actor.
d No, they're ______ doctors.
e I'm ______ lawyer.
f No, she's ______ journalist.
g They're ______ engineers.
h Yes, they're ______ students.

b What's my job? Read the texts and complete the sentences.

1 "I work inside and outside, and I work during the day or at night. I drive a car or a motorcycle, and sometimes I walk along the street. I don't earn a lot of money. I wear a uniform."

He's ______________________.

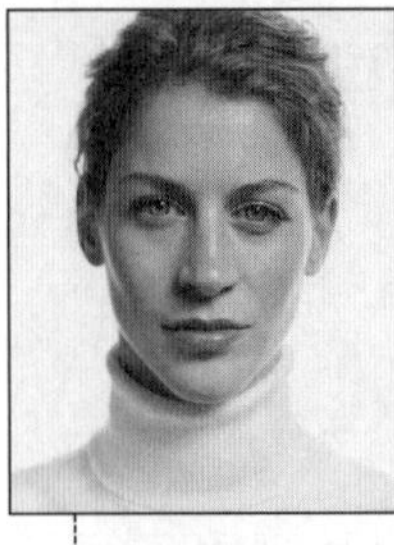

2 "I work in an office with a computer or outside with other people. I speak other languages, and I sometimes travel to different countries. I don't wear a uniform. I work for a newspaper."

She's ______________________.

3 "I wear a uniform, and I work with other people. I have special qualifications, but I don't earn a lot of money. I work during the day or at night, but I don't work outside. I work in a hospital."

She's ______________________.

3 PRONUNCIATION consonant sounds

a Write the words in the chart.

China ~~**sh**op~~ **ph**oto **y**ou **ch**air **G**ermany **j**ob **f**ile E**ng**land **u**niversity dri**n**k **p**erson

p parrot	f flower	tʃ chess	dʒ jazz	y yacht	ŋ singer
shop	______	______	______	______	______
______	______	______	______	______	______

b Underline the stressed syllable in these words.

1 journalist 4 pilot 7 salesperson
2 politician 5 musician 8 housewife
3 hairdresser 6 engineer 9 student

c Practice saying the words in **a** and **b**.

More Words to Learn

Write translations and try to remember the words.

Word	Pronunciation	Translation
factory *noun*	/ˈfæktəri/	
hands *noun*	/hændz/	
other *adjective*	/ˈʌðər/	
earn *verb*	/ərn/	
relax *verb*	/rɪˈlæks/	
normally *adverb*	/ˈnɔrməli/	
together *adverb*	/təˈgeðər/	
inside *adverb*	/ɪnˈsaɪd/	
outside *adverb*	/aʊtˈsaɪd/	
It depends	/ɪt dɪˈpɛndz/	

QUESTION TIME

Can you answer these questions?

1 What do you do?
2 Where do you work or study?
3 What does your father do?
4 What does your mother do?
5 In your country, what jobs are well–paid?

Study Link MultiROM

I want to be the white man's brother, not his brother-in-law.
Martin Luther King, American civil rights activist

2D Relatively famous

1 GRAMMAR possessive *s*

a Order the words to make sentences.

1 house / Miami / sister's / in / My / is
My sister's house is in Miami.

2 works / her / in / Barbara / store / brother's
______________________________________.

3 Japanese / Her / car / boyfriend's / is
______________________________________.

4 father / you / Do / know / Jennifer's
______________________________________?

5 from / girlfriend / Brazil / brother's / is / My
______________________________________.

6 daughter's / bank / in / friend / Our / works / a
______________________________________.

7 job / stressful / Is / Tom's / very
______________________________________?

8 money / mother / lot / earns / of / Susan's / a
______________________________________.

b Correct the sentences. Add an apostrophe (').

1 Martha is my brothers girlfriend.
Martha is my brother's girlfriend.

2 This is my parents car.
This is my parents' car.

3 Do you know Kathys brother ?
______________________________________?

4 The womens restroom is over there.
______________________________________.

5 I think this is that womans bag.
______________________________________.

6 Our teachers wife is French.
______________________________________.

7 We have coffee in the Teachers Room at 10:00.
______________________________________.

c Look at the *'s* in these sentences. Write a letter in the box: A = possessive, B = *is*.

1 My father's apartment is downtown. [*A*]
2 His name's Robert. [*B*]
3 Phillip's brother is an actor. [ ]
4 My son's wife likes animals. [ ]
5 His brother's very nice. [ ]
6 Clare's children work in Chicago. [ ]
7 Our mother's 50 today. [ ]
8 Their father's an engineer. [ ]

Study Link **Student Book p.124** *Grammar Bank 2D*

2 VOCABULARY the family

a Complete the chart.

grandmother	*grandfather*
	father
aunt	
	husband
sister	
	son
niece	
	cousin

b Complete the sentences.

1 My mother's sister is my *aunt*.
2 My brother's son is my __________.
3 My father's brother is my __________.
4 My mother's father is my __________.
5 My uncle's son is my __________.
6 My sister's daughter is my __________.

Study Link **Student Book p.145** *Vocabulary Bank*

3 PRONUNCIATION consonant sounds

Write the words in the chart. Practice saying them.

~~book~~ housewife think brother nurse this
matches three men builder nephew have

b	θ	ð	m	n	h
bag	**th**umb	mo**th**er	**m**onkey	**n**ose	**h**ouse
book	______	______	______	______	______
______	______	______	______	______	______

4 READING

The Rainforest Children

John Allen is 43 years old, and he has four children: two daughters and two sons. John is a plant scientist, and he lives with three of his children in the South American rainforest. Their "house" is a group of tents near the River Orinoco in Venezuela. John's wife and one of his daughters prefer to live in London.

John's children don't go to school because John is their teacher. He teaches them everything he knows, including how to survive in South America.

The children don't know how to use a PlayStation™, but they can all drive, even his 9-year-old son, Simon. At night they drive their car 50 yards from the kitchen tent to the bedroom tent because there are a lot of wild animals in the area. They spend their free time playing and reading books, and in the evening they listen to the news on the radio. They don't have a TV or a CD player. In the summer the children's friends come from London to visit. When they go home, they tell their parents incredible stories of their vacation in the Venezuelan rainforest.

a Write T (True) or F (False).

1. John is a biology teacher. *F*
2. John's four children live in Venezuela. ___
3. They live in a house. ___
4. John teaches the children in a school. ___
5. The children don't play computer games. ___
6. Simon doesn't drive. ___
7. They don't watch TV. ___
8. The children's friends visit with their parents. ___

b Look at the highlighted words. What do you think they mean? Check your dictionary.

More Words to Learn

Write translations and try to remember the words.

Word	Pronunciation	Translation
relatives *noun*	/ˈrɛlətɪvz/	
possessions *noun*	/pəˈzɛʃnz/	
shoes *noun*	/ʃuz/	
hat *noun*	/hæt/	
cap *noun*	/kæp/	
Which? *pronoun*	/wɪtʃ/	
Who? *pronoun*	/hu/	
How many? *quantifier*	/haʊ ˈmɛni/	

QUESTION TIME

Can you answer these questions?

1. How many brothers and sisters do you have?
2. Where do your grandparents live?
3. What's your mother's first name?
4. Do you have any cousins?
5. Do you live in your parents' house?

Study Link MultiROM

CAN YOU REMEMBER...? FILES 1&2

Complete each sentence with one word.

1. Hello, Gary. How ______ your mother?
2. My girlfriend's from Paris. She's ______.
3. Martin's English, and ______ wife's American.
4. Please ______ off your cell phone.
5. That man ______ four different languages.
6. **A** ______ you smoke?
   B No, I don't.
7. Her father's ______ engineer.
8. My sister's ______ is my niece.

Study Link www.oup.com/elt/americanenglishfile/1

1 VOCABULARY hotel words

Complete the words.

1 the *reception*
2 the e________
3 the b________
4 the f________ f________
5 a d________ room
6 a s________ room

2 CHECKING IN

Complete the conversation with a phrase from the box.

Here you are. ~~I have a reservation.~~ It's OK.
Non-smoking, please. That's right. Where's the elevator?

A Good evening, madam.
B Hello. 1 *I have a reservation.* My name's Melissa Grant.
A For two nights?
B Yes. 2 ________
A Can I see your passport, please?
B Just a moment. 3 ________
A Do you want a smoking or non-smoking room?
B 4 ________
A Here's your key. It's room 212 – on the second floor.
B Thank you. 5 ________
A It's over there. Do you need help with your bags?
B No, thanks. 6 ________

3 SOCIAL ENGLISH

Complete the sentences with the missing words.

A 1 *Would* you like another drink?
B No, I 2 h________ to go now. It's late. Sorry.
A 3 T________ OK. It's no problem. 4 S________ you tomorrow.
B Yes, 5 g________. Sleep well.

4 READING

a Match the hotels and the guests. Write the numbers in the boxes.

1 A lawyer and his friend want to spend a weekend in Oxford to walk, talk, and play golf.
2 A company director wants to have a two-day meeting in Oxford with managers from other European offices.
3 A family with a dog wants to travel to Scotland, but they want to stay the night in Oxford because their journey is too long for one day.

Hotels in Oxford

Westwood Country Hotel
Hinksey Hill Top, Oxford OX1 5BG
- 14 double rooms, 6 single rooms
- Parking lot
- Restaurant
- Bar
- Cable / satellite television
- Near golf course

Old Black Horse Hotel
102 St Clements, Oxford OX4 1AR
- 9 double rooms, 1 single room
- Restaurant
- Parking lot
- Television
- Pets welcome
- Near highway

The Randolph
Beaumont Street, Oxford OX1 2LN
- 7 suites, 63 doubles, 39 singles
- Conference center
- 24-hour room service
- Cable / satellite TV
- Parking lot
- Restaurant
- 50 miles from airport

b Underline five words or phrases you don't know. Use your dictionary to look up their meaning and pronunciation.

Soccer? It's the beautiful game.
Pelé, Brazilian soccer player

3A Pretty woman

1 VOCABULARY common adjectives

a Complete the crossword.

b Write the colors.

1 red + green = *brown*
2 black + white = ____________
3 red + yellow = ____________
4 white + red = ____________
5 blue + yellow = ____________

Study Link Student Book p.146 *Vocabulary Bank*

2 PRONUNCIATION vowel sounds

a Circle the word with a different vowel sound.

i	u	aɪ	oʊ	ɛ
cheap	study	high	comb	red
niece	blue	dry	book	pen
eat	new	big	slow	me
(wear)	do	wife	no	wet

b Underline the stressed syllable in these words.

1 beautiful 3 expensive 5 ugly
2 empty 4 difficult 6 dirty

c Practice saying the words in **a** and **b**.

3 GRAMMAR adjectives

Order the words to make sentences.

1 has / boyfriend / rich / Cathy / a
Cathy has a rich boyfriend.
2 expensive / drives / Jack / car / an
______________________________.
3 lipstick / wears / Helen / red
______________________________.
4 a / house / live / parents / in / very / My / big
______________________________.
5 Saturdays / a / I / lunch / cook / on / big
______________________________.
6 don't / days / like / I / wet
______________________________.
7 very / 's / My / grandfather / old
______________________________.
8 children / hair / have / Paula's / black
______________________________.

Study Link Student Book p.126 *Grammar Bank 3A*

4 VOCABULARY appearance, *very*

a Match the pictures and the sentences. Write the letter in the box.

1 He's very tall and he has short, dark hair. *e*
2 He's heavy, with long, dark hair. ☐
3 She's old and heavy with short, blond hair. ☐
4 She's young, tall, and she has dark hair. ☐
5 He's young. He's tall and thin with short hair. ☐
6 She's short and thin, and she has long hair. ☐

b Complete with an expression from the box.

I'm cold. I'm hot. I'm sad. ~~I'm angry.~~
I'm tired. I'm thirsty. I'm hungry. I'm happy.

1 My friend is very late. *I'm angry.*
2 It's 2°C. ______
3 It's my birthday! ______
4 It's 85°F. ______
5 It's time for lunch. ______
6 My boyfriend doesn't love me. ______
7 I want a glass of water. ______
8 It's very late. ______

Study Link **Student Book p.146** *Vocabulary Bank*

5 READING

Who is the perfect Bond girl?

There are 20 Bond films in the "Bond, James Bond" exhibition at the Science Museum in London. In these films, James Bond has 41 girlfriends, but they are all different. Some have brown hair, some have blond hair, some have dark hair, and some have red hair. But experts now know exactly what type of girl James Bond likes. They say Bond's typical girlfriend has brown hair and brown eyes. She is tall (1m 70), thin and, of course, very beautiful. And who is the perfect Bond girl? They say it's Diana Rigg in the film *On Her Majesty's Secret Service*.

Adapted from a website

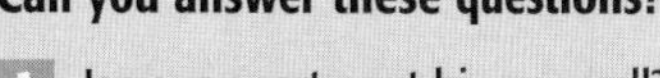

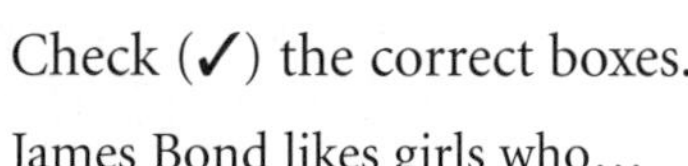

Check (✓) the correct boxes.

James Bond likes girls who…

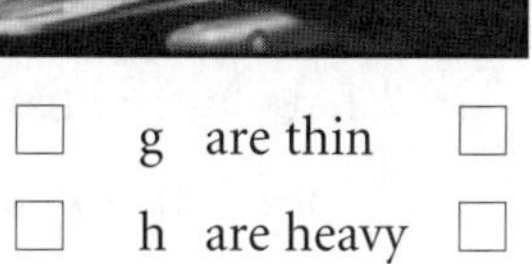

a are rich ☐ d are beautiful ☐ g are thin ☐
b are short ☐ e have blue eyes ☐ h are heavy ☐
c are tall ☐ f have brown eyes ☐

More Words to Learn

Write translations and try to remember the words.

Word	Pronunciation	Translation
president *noun*	/ˈprɛzədənt/	
airline *noun*	/ˈɛrlaɪn/	
clothes *noun*	/kloʊz/	
moon *noun*	/mun/	
hair *noun*	/hɛr/	
good-looking *adjective*	/gʊdˈlʊkɪŋ/	
pretty *adjective*	/ˈprɪti/	
feel *verb*	/fil/	
separate *verb*	/ˈsɛprət/	
another *determiner*	/əˈnʌðər/	

QUESTION TIME

Can you answer these questions?

1 Is your apartment big or small?
2 Are you tall or short?
3 What color hair do you have?
4 Are you hungry?
5 Are restaurants cheap or expensive in your country?

Study Link **MultiROM**

3 o'clock is always too late or too early for anything you want to do.
Jean-Paul Sartre, French philosopher

Wake up, get out of bed...

1 GRAMMAR telling the time

Write the times.

1 *It's twenty to six.* 2 ______

3 ______ 4 ______

5 ______ 6 ______

7 ______ 8 ______

Study Link Student Book p.126 *Grammar Bank 3B*

2 PRONUNCIATION the letter *o*

Circle the word with a different vowel sound. Practice saying the words.

ɑ	u	ʌ	oʊ
n**o**t	sch**oo**l	n**o**	sl**ow**
(h**o**me)	tw**o**	s**o**n	g**o**
sh**o**p	f**oo**d	m**o**ther	c**o**mb
j**o**b	h**o**t	fr**o**m	br**ow**n

3 VOCABULARY daily routine

a Complete the phrases with *go, get, take,* or *have.*

1 *get*	dressed	5 ___	breakfast	9 ___	to bed
2 ___	to the gym	6 ___	to work	10 ___	up
3 ___	shopping	7 ___	a shower	11 ___	to work
4 ___	a coffee	8 ___	home	12 ___	dinner

b Circle the action which you usually do first.

1 get dressed / (take a shower)
2 get up / wake up
3 make dinner / have dinner
4 sleep / go to bed
5 go home / get home
6 start work / get to work
7 have lunch / have breakfast
8 have dinner / have a coffee

Study Link Student Book p.147 *Vocabulary Bank*

4 GRAMMAR the time, daily routine

a Complete the sentences with *have*, *go*, *take*, or *get*.

A housewife's life is very stressful – or is it?

Many people think that housewives have a very stressful life. We ask two, Maggie and Eve, about their typical day.

First Maggie Macallan, from Quebec, Canada.

"I [1] *get* up at 7:30, and I make breakfast for my children. Then I [2]______ dressed and take the children to school. Then I [3]______ shopping. I go to the supermarket and buy food and things for the house. When I [4]______ home, I make the beds and clean the house. I [5]______ a shower before I pick up the children from school at four o'clock. In the evening we [6]______ dinner and watch television. I [7]______ to bed at 10:30 because I'm very tired."

Eve Standish is from Houston, Texas.

"I [8]______ up at ten o'clock and [9]______ fruit and orange juice for breakfast. Then I [10]______ a bath and get dressed. At 11:30, I meet my friends downtown. First, we [11]______ a coffee, and then we [12]______ shopping. We usually [13]______ lunch at about one o'clock in a restaurant in town. In the afternoon, we sometimes [14]______ to the gym. When I [15]______ home, I [16]______ a drink with my husband. In the evening we [17]______ to the theater or to a nightclub. I normally [18]______ to bed very late."

b Write questions about Maggie or Eve.

1 What time *does Maggie get up*?
She gets up at 7:30.

2 *Does Eve have breakfast*?
Yes, she does. She has fruit and orange juice.

3 ______ in the morning?
No, she doesn't. She takes a shower in the afternoon.

4 Where ______?
She meets her friends downtown.

5 What ______?
She has dinner and watches television.

6 What time ______?
She goes to bed at 10:30.

7 ______?
No, she doesn't. She goes to bed late.

More Words to Learn

Write translations and try to remember the words.

Word	Pronunciation	Translation
cup (of coffee) *noun*	/kʌp/	
expert *noun*	/'ɛkspərt/	
same *adjective*	/seɪm/	
invite *verb*	/ɪn'vaɪt/	
ride *verb*	/raɪd/	
pick up *verb*	/pɪk ʌp/	
guide *noun*	/gaɪd/	
more *quantifier*	/mɔr/	
all *quantifier*	/ɔl/	
because *conjunction*	/bɪ'kɔz/	

Study idea

1 Use a highlighter pen to highlight words that are difficult to remember (in your Student Book and Workbook).

2 Cover the **Word** column (above) and test your memory. Which words are difficult for you to remember? Highlight them.

QUESTION TIME

Can you answer these questions?

1 What time do you get up?
2 What do you have for breakfast?
3 Where do you have lunch?
4 How do you get to work or school?
5 What time do you go to bed?

Study Link **MultiROM**

The man who works and is not bored is never old.
Pablo Casals, Spanish cellist

The island with a secret

1 GRAMMAR adverbs of frequency

a Complete the **You** column in the chart. Then complete the sentences with a verb and an adverb of frequency.

always ✓✓✓✓✓ usually ✓✓✓✓ often ✓✓✓ sometimes ✓✓ hardly ever ✓ never –	Steffi	Robert	You
eat fruit and vegetables	✓✓	✓✓✓✓✓	
play sports or exercise	–	✓✓✓	
be relaxed	✓✓✓✓	✓✓✓✓	
drink alcohol	✓✓✓	✓	
be sick	✓✓✓	✓	

1 Steffi *sometimes eats* fruit and vegetables.
2 She __________ sports or exercises.
3 She __________ relaxed.
4 She __________ alcohol.
5 She __________ sick.

6 Robert __________ fruit and vegetables.
7 He __________ sports or exercises.
8 He __________ relaxed.
9 He __________ alcohol.
10 He __________ sick.

11 I __________ fruit and vegetables.
12 I __________ sports or exercises.
13 I __________ relaxed.
14 I __________ alcohol.
15 I __________ sick.

Who lives the Okinawa way?

b Write the adverb of frequency in the correct place in the sentence.

1 Tom rides his motorcycle to work. (sometimes)
Tom sometimes rides his motorcycle to work.
2 My boyfriend is late. (never)
__________.
3 The children walk to school. (usually)
__________.
4 I'm hungry. (always)
__________.
5 Teachers are stressed. (often)
__________.
6 I see my uncle and aunt. (hardly ever)
__________.
7 Professional soccer players are rich. (usually)
__________.
8 Pilots sleep in hotels. (often)
__________.

Study Link **Student Book p.126** *Grammar Bank 3C*

2 VOCABULARY "Okinawa" reading

Complete the sentences.

stay at home popular meat unusual beach
sunset ~~rice~~ busy take my time

1 Chinese people eat a lot of *rice*.
2 The secretary is very __________ – she has a lot of work.
3 That restaurant is __________ because the food is good.
4 The opposite of *usual* is __________.
5 I like to __________! I don't like to be in a hurry.
6 In the summer, I go to the __________ every day.
7 I love the __________ when the sky is orange and red.
8 Vegetarians don't eat __________.
9 I don't want to go out tonight. I want to __________.

3 VOCABULARY time words and expressions

a Answer the questions.

1	How many minutes are in an hour?	*sixty*
2	How many months are in a year?	
3	How many days are in a week?	
4	How many seconds are in a minute?	
5	How many weeks are in a month?	
6	How many hours are in a day?	
7	How many days are in June?	
8	How many weeks are in a year?	

b Complete the sentences with one word.

1 Nurses sometimes work all week and on weekends.
Nurses sometimes work *every* day.

2 Jon usually goes on vacation in March, May, and July.
Jon usually goes on vacation ________ times a year.

3 I have English classes on Tuesdays and Thursdays.
I have English classes twice a ________.

4 Katia goes shopping on Friday.
Katia goes shopping ________ a week.

5 Liz takes her dog for a walk at 7:00 a.m. and at 6:00 p.m.
Liz takes her dog for a walk ________ a day.

6 I buy a new pair of sunglasses in the summer.
I buy a new pair of sunglasses once a ________.

Study Link **Student Book p.148** *Vocabulary Bank*

4 PRONUNCIATION the letter *h*

a Match the word to the pronunciation.

1 half	e	a /hɪr/
2 high	☐	b /ˈaʊər/
3 how	☐	c /haɪ/
4 hour	☐	d /ˈhəri/
5 hardly	☐	e /hæf/
6 here	☐	f /ˈhæpi/
7 hurry	☐	g /ˈhɑrdli/
8 happy	☐	h /haʊ/

In which word is the *h* not pronounced?

b Practice saying the words.

More Words to Learn

Write translations and try to remember the words.

Word	Pronunciation	Translation
island *noun*	/ˈaɪlənd/	
mile *noun*	/maɪl/	
vegetables *noun*	/ˈvɛdʒtəblz/	
fruit *noun*	/frut/	
(un)usual *adjective*	/ˈyuʒuəl/	
traditional *adjective*	/trəˈdɪʃnl/	
(un)healthy *adjective*	/ˈhɛlθi/	
sick *adjective*	/sɪk/	
until *conjunction*	/ənˈtɪl/	
a long time	/ə lɔŋ taɪm/	

QUESTION TIME

Can you answer these questions?

1 How often are you in a hurry?
2 How often do you exercise?
3 How often do you go to English class?
4 How often do you eat meat?
5 How often do you go to the movies?

Study Link **MultiROM**

Time is a great teacher, but unfortunately it kills all its pupils.
Hector Louis Berlioz, French composer

3D On the last Wednesday in August

1 VOCABULARY the date

a Continue the series.

1 January, February, *March*, *April*
2 May, July, ________, ________
3 September, October, ________, ________
4 March, June, ________, ________
5 spring, summer, ________, ________
6 first, second, ________, ________
7 sixth, eighth, ________, ________
8 fifth, tenth, ________, ________

b Complete the chart.

1/1 ~~2/14~~ 7/4 10/31 12/25

Day	Date	You say…
Valentine's Day	*2/14*	*February fourteenth*
Christmas Day		
US Independence Day		
Halloween		
New Year's Day		

Study Link Student Book p.148 *Vocabulary Bank*

2 PRONUNCIATION vowel sounds, word stress

a Write the words in the chart.

first **sec**ond ~~fall~~ July April
Novem**ber** **nin**th May **Au**gust thi**r**d

ɔ	ər	ɛ	eɪ	aɪ
fall	______	______	______	______
______	______	______	______	______

b Underline the stressed syllable in these words.

1 January	5 May	9 September
2 February	6 June	10 October
3 March	7 July	11 November
4 April	8 August	12 December

c Practice saying the words in **a** and **b**.

3 GRAMMAR prepositions of time

a Write the words in the correct column.

~~February~~ ~~November 5th~~ ~~5:30~~ the weekend
Sunday the morning the fall
Friday afternoon September 22nd night
3 o'clock 2010 lunchtime noon 1966

in	on	at
February	*November 5th*	*5:30*

b Complete the sentences with prepositions of time.

"My name is Nunzia Manfredini and I work for a publicity agency. I usually get up [1] *at* six o'clock [2] ____ Mondays, Wednesdays, and Fridays because I have my English class before I start work. [3] ____ Tuesdays and Thursdays I get up later. I go to work by train, but [4] ____ Fridays I drive my car, so I can visit my mother [5] ____ the afternoon. When the class finishes [6] ____ quarter to nine, I go to my office. I have lunch [7] ____ two o'clock. Then I work until about seven o'clock. [8] ____ the summer, I work different hours because [9] ____ June 15th we change to the summer schedule. It's very hot in Rome [10] ____ August, so most people go on vacation!"

Study Link Student Book p.126 *Grammar Bank 3D*

4 READING

a Match the questions to the paragraphs.

Where do people stay? Where is it?
How do people get there? When is it?
~~What is the Kumbh Mela bathing festival?~~

The Kumbh Mela bathing festival

1 *What is the Kumbh Mela bathing festival?*

The Kumbh Mela bathing festival is a ceremony for Hindus where they celebrate their religion. They go to the River Ganges to clean their bodies. Millions of Indian people take part in the ceremony, and it is impossible to move in the streets near the river.

2 ______________________________

The festival takes place in one of four cities in India. The cities are Ujjain, Haridwar, Nasik, and Allahabad.

3 ______________________________

The Kumbh Mela does not happen on a fixed date, but it takes place every three years, in April or May. The exact dates depend on the stars.

4 ______________________________

There are special trains that take people to the Kumbh Mela from all over India. During the festival the trains are very full.

5 ______________________________

People usually stay at camps where they eat and sleep. The food is vegetarian because Hindus do not eat meat or eggs.

b Highlight five words you don't know. What do you think they mean? Check your dictionary.

More Words to Learn

Write translations and try to remember the words.

Word	Pronunciation	Translation
birthday *noun*	/ˈbərθdeɪ/	
the beginning *noun*	/ðə bɪˈgɪnɪŋ/	
the middle *noun*	/ðə ˈmɪdl/	
favorite *adjective*	/ˈfeɪvrət/	
continue *verb*	/kənˈtɪnyu/	
want *verb*	/wɑnt/	
change *verb*	/tʃeɪndʒ/	
also *adverb*	/ˈɔlsoʊ/	
during *preposition*	/ˈdʊrɪŋ/	
in front of *preposition*	/ɪn frʌnt əv/	

QUESTION TIME

Can you answer these questions?

1. When's your birthday?
2. When's your mother's birthday?
3. What's your favorite month?
4. What's your favorite season?
5. When do you usually relax?

Study Link MultiROM

CAN YOU REMEMBER...? FILES 2&3

Complete each sentence with one word.

1. Jim __________ like dogs, but he likes cats.
2. __________ your boyfriend live near here?
3. Nurses always __________ a uniform.
4. My __________ husband is my uncle.
5. I want a drink. I'm __________.
6. We get up at half __________ six.
7. **A** How __________ do you go to English classes?
   B Twice a week.
8. They go to bed late __________ the weekend.

3 In a coffee shop

PRACTICAL ENGLISH

1 VOCABULARY coffee and snacks

Complete the words.

1 *cappuccino*
2 f_______ c_______
3 e_______
4 c_______ c_______ c_______
5 b_______

2 BUYING A COFFEE

a Complete the missing words in these phrases.

1 *Do* you have any desserts?
2 Here y_______ are. Thanks.
3 To g_______.
4 How m_______ is that?
5 C_______ I have an espresso, please?
6 Regular, p_______.
7 A chocolate chip c_______, please.

b Put the sentences from exercise **a** in the dialogue below. Write a number in each box.

A Next, please. **B** *5*
A Regular or large? **B** ☐
A Anything else? **B** ☐
A Brownies or chocolate chip cookies. **B** ☐
A To have here or to go? **B** ☐
A Here you are. **B** ☐
A That's $3.40, please. **B** ☐

3 SOCIAL ENGLISH

Complete the dialogue with these words.

sorry over free ~~welcome~~ worry

A Thanks for the coffee, Alan.
B You're [1] *welcome*.
A Look, there's a [2]_______ table [3]_______ there.
B Oh no! The coffee. It's all over your shirt! I'm really [4]_______.
A Don't [5]_______. It's OK.

4 READING

a Read the descriptions of the coffee shops.

Coffee shops

a BATTERY PARK

Battery Park is more than a coffee shop – it also serves a selection of fruit juices, snacks, and homemade desserts. Customers can sit inside on comfortable sofas in the winter or outside on the terrace in the summer.

b BAMBOO CAFE

Apart from its excellent coffee, you can try a variety of eastern and western food here. The menu isn't expensive and the desserts are delicious.

c CAFE POP

This stylish coffee shop serves all kinds of hot and cold drinks and some fantastic snacks. However, its most interesting feature is the decoration – the walls are covered with pictures of pop stars from the 90s.

d KAFKA'S

Kafka's coffee shop is part of a bookstore, so you can take a book from the shelves and sit in a comfortable chair to look at it. The coffee is great, and snacks are also served.

e LES DÉLICES DE CHAMPAGNE

This coffee shop is famous for its desserts and ice creams, and they do a very special breakfast. However, it's very expensive, so only come here if it's your birthday or if a friend is paying!

b In which coffee shop can you…

1 …read a book while you drink your coffee? *d*
2 …enjoy your coffee in the sun? ☐
3 …spend a lot of money on your coffee? ☐
4 …have food from different countries? ☐
5 …see pictures of famous musicians? ☐

c Underline five words or phrases you don't know. Use your dictionary to look up their meaning and pronunciation.

I can't dance

Can't act, slightly bald, also dances.
Said after Fred Astaire's first audition

1 GRAMMAR *can* / *can't* (ability)

a Write a sentence for each picture.

1 *He can't play the guitar.*

2 ______________________.

3 ______________.

4 ______________.

5 ______________.

b Write a question for each picture. Then write your answer: *Yes, I can.* or *No, I can't.*

			Your answer
1	*Can* you	*play the guitar*?	__________
2	______ you	______________?	__________
3	______ you	______________?	__________
4	______ you	______________?	__________
5	______ you	______________?	__________

Study Link **Student Book p.128** *Grammar Bank 4A*

2 PRONUNCIATION sentence stress

a Underline the stressed words.

1 **A** Can you speak German?
B Yes, I can.

2 I can't find the keys.

3 She can sing.

4 Where can I buy a newspaper?

5 **A** Can your father cook?
B No, he can't.

6 My sister can't swim.

b Practice saying the sentences.

3 VOCABULARY more verb phrases

a Complete the crossword.

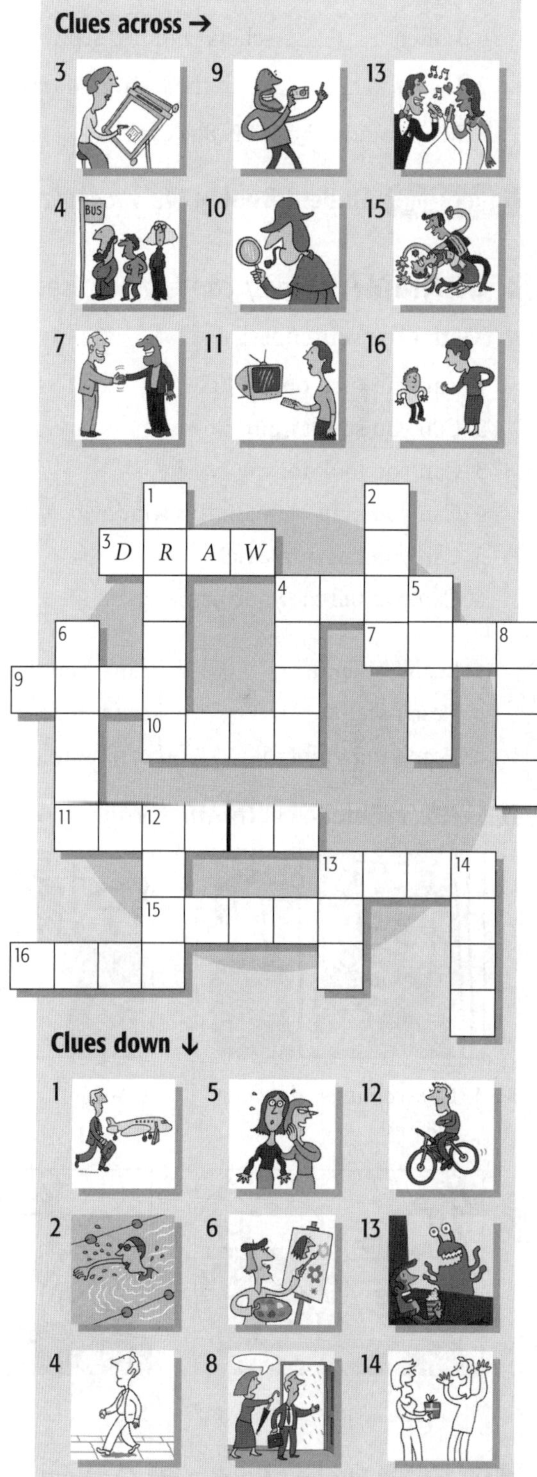

b Complete the sentences.

turn off	call	help	see
hear	play	~~buy~~	run

1 I *buy* a newspaper every day.

2 I ________ a taxi when I'm in a hurry.

3 He wants to ________ a movie this evening.

4 Please ________ the TV when you go to bed.

5 Please ________ me. I don't understand this.

6 I often ________ chess with my nephew.

7 I want to ________ in the Boston Marathon this year.

8 My grandmother's 92. She can't ________ very well.

Study Link **Student Book p.149** *Vocabulary Bank*

4 GRAMMAR *can / can't* (other uses)

a Match the sentences.

1 Can you turn on the light? [*b*]

2 Can you speak more slowly? [ ]

3 Can you look for my keys? [ ]

4 Can you help me with this window? [ ]

5 Can you hurry, please? [ ]

6 Can you tell me your name again? [ ]

a I can't open it.

b I can't see.

c I can't remember it.

d I can't find them.

e I can't understand you.

f I can't wait.

b Write a sentence with *can* or *can't* for each picture.

1 *Can you open the door, please?*

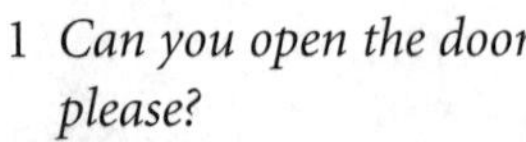

2 You ________________.

3 ________ pass the sugar?

4 I ________________.

Study Link **Student Book p.128** *Grammar Bank 4A*

More Words to Learn

Write translations and try to remember the words.

Word	Pronunciation	Translation
advertisement *noun*	/ædvər'taɪzmənt/	
(pop) star *noun*	/stɑr/	
map *noun*	/mæp/	
(TV) channel *noun*	/'tʃænl/	
program *noun / verb*	/'proʊgræm/	
creative *adjective*	/kri'eɪtɪv/	
athletic *adjective*	/æθ'lɛtɪk/	
practical *adjective*	/'præktɪkl/	
follow *verb*	/'fɑloʊ/	
need *verb*	/nid/	

Study idea

1 Look at the **Pronunciation** column in **More Words to Learn.** Remember that this mark (') = the stress is on the next syllable.

2 Underline the stressed syllables in the **Word** column. Practice saying the words.

3 Remember to underline the stress when you write down new words.

QUESTION TIME

Can you answer these questions?

1 Can you play a musical instrument?

2 Can you drive?

3 Can you dance well?

4 What sports can you play?

5 Can you take good photos?

Study Link **MultiROM**

Study Link www.oup.com/elt/americanenglishfile/1

People who say money can't buy you happiness
don't know where to go shopping.
Anonymous

Shopping – men love it!

1 GRAMMAR *like* (+ verb + *-ing*)

a Write the verb + *-ing* in the correct column.

~~wait~~	come	take	get	dance	find
buy	run	swim	draw	give	stop

verb + *-ing*	~~e~~ + *-ing*	double consonant + *-ing*
waiting		

b Look at the chart with the results of a class survey. Complete the sentences.

☺☺ = love ☹ = don't like ☺ = like ☹☹ = hate	Women	Men
watch soccer	☹☹	☺☺
dance at parties	☺	☹
buy presents	☺	☹☹
have lunch with their mother	☺☺	☺
play chess	☹	☺

1 Women *hate watching* soccer.
   Men *love watching* soccer.
2 Women ________________ at parties.
   Men ________________ at parties.
3 Women ________________ presents.
   Men ________________ presents.
4 Women ________________ lunch with their mother.
   Men ________________ lunch with their mother.
5 Women ________________ chess.
   Men ________________ chess.

Study Link **Student Book p.128** *Grammar Bank 4B*

2 PRONUNCIATION /ŋ/

Practice saying these sentences with the /ŋ/ sound.

1 I hate goi**ng** to the ba**n**k.
2 Tha**n**ks for buyi**ng** me the pi**n**k dress.
3 My u**n**cle loves goi**ng** for lo**ng** walks.
4 Do you thi**n**k she si**ng**s good so**ng**s?

3 VOCABULARY free-time activities

a Write the verb.

ride	read	~~take~~	go	talk	play

1 *take* photos your umbrella the dog for a walk
2 ________ home to bed shopping
3 ________ chess computer games the guitar
4 ________ a map music a book
5 ________ to a friend on the phone fast
6 ________ a horse a motorcycle a bike

b Complete the activities with a verb + *-ing*.

exercising	listening	~~watching~~	playing	reading
dancing	shopping	going	meeting	using

Top 10 free-time activities

1	*watching*	TV
2		friends
3		a computer
4		to the movies
5		a book or the newspaper
6		soccer (or another sport)
7		to music
8		at a nightclub
9		(at the gym)
10		for clothes

Come to Center Parcs

Adapted from a website

Center Parcs is the perfect family holiday. There are four of them in England and you can do almost anything you want there.

If it's exercise you want, you can go walking or cycling through the forest. There are also adventure sports like windsurfing. If you're a team player, you can play basketball, tennis, or soccer. But if you prefer quieter activities, you can do tai chi or yoga in the gym, or go swimming in the numerous swimming pools. And if you don't like exercising at all, you can learn to paint in the art class or just sit in the cafe and relax.

Center Parcs isn't only for adults; children enjoy it as much as their parents. Mothers and fathers can relax in the sauna or play golf while babies and small children play with their friends in the Time Out clubs.

There is something for everyone at Center Parcs.

a Write T (true) or F (false).

1 There is only one Center Parc in England. F
2 Center Parcs isn't only for children. ___
3 Center Parcs is in the city. ___
4 Center Parcs is only good if you like sports. ___

b Check ✓ the activities people do at Center Parcs.

1 riding bikes	☐	6 soccer	☐
2 painting	☐	7 shopping	☐
3 learning a language	☐	8 yoga	☐
4 doing housework	☐	9 swimming	☐
5 relaxing	☐	10 windsurfing	☐

More Words to Learn

Write translations and try to remember the words.

Word	Pronunciation	Translation
store *noun*	/stɔr/	
shop *verb / noun*	/ʃɑp/	
hobby *noun*	/ˈhɑbi/	
toys *noun*	/tɔɪz/	
try on *verb*	/traɪ ɑn/	
decide *verb*	/dɪˈsaɪd/	
possibly *adverb*	/ˈpɑsəbli/	
today *adverb*	/təˈdeɪ/	
some *quantifier*	/səm/	
everything *pronoun*	/ˈɛvriθɪŋ/	

QUESTION TIME

Can you answer these questions?

1 Do you like shopping?
2 How often do you buy clothes?
3 Do you like going to the supermarket?
4 What do you hate doing during the week?
5 What do you like doing on the weekend?

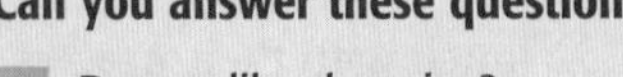

Study Link MultiROM

Study Link www.oup.com/elt/americanenglishfile/1

A man falls in love through his eyes, a woman through her ears.
Woodrow Wyatt, American writer

Fatal attraction?

1 GRAMMAR object pronouns

a Complete the chart.

Subject pronouns	Object pronouns
I	*me*
	you
he	
she	
	it
we	
	you
they	

b Complete the sentences with object pronouns.

1 I love you. Do you love *me*?
2 I work with John. I have lunch with ______ every day.
3 Can you speak more slowly? I can't understand ______.
4 She lives near me. I often see ______ on the bus.
5 She doesn't like my sisters. She never speaks to ______.
6 This music's terrible. I hate ______.
7 **A** What do you think of these boots?
B I don't like ______ very much.
8 I want to talk to you about something. Can you call ______ tomorrow, please?
9 We arrive at the airport at 8:00. Can you meet ______ there?
10 Excuse me, I have a problem. Can you help ______?

c Complete the text with these words.

he him she she her ~~they~~ they them

David, Anna, Peter, and Vicky are all friends. [1] *They* live together in a big apartment, but [2] ______ have some problems. David loves Anna, but [3] ______ doesn't love [4] ______. Anna loves Peter, but [5] ______ doesn't love [6] ______. David and Peter don't like Vicky, and [7] ______ doesn't like [8] ______.

David
Anna
Peter
Vicky

Study Link **Student Book p.128** *Grammar Bank 4C*

2 VOCABULARY "love stories" reading

a Complete the text with these words.

leave ~~fall in love~~ go out together meet come back get married

Do you love me?

- ♥ About 75% of people [1] *fall in love* with a friend from school.
- ♥ 15% of people [2] ______ a new partner when they go away on vacation.
- ♥ 30% of couples [3] ______ for a year or more before they start living together.
- ♥ Only about 10% [4] ______ to this person.
- ♥ Sadly, 25% [5] ______ their first husband or wife in the first two years.
- ♥ About 5% [6] ______ because they can't find another partner.

b Match sentences a–h to the picture story.

Music…the food of love

a After the concert, they go out to dinner together.

b ~~Two students meet at music school in Toronto.~~

c They live together in Australia.

d Five years later, he goes on vacation to Sydney. He goes to a concert at the Sydney Opera House, and she is one of the singers.

e She doesn't write to him.

f They fall in love and go out together.

g He asks her to marry him and she says, "Yes."

h When they finish music school, she goes home to Australia.

3 PRONUNCIATION /ɪ/ and /i/

~~r**i**ch~~	b**ui**lder	pol**i**ce	spr**i**ng	k**ey**	l**ea**ve
gr**ee**n	polit**i**cian	th**i**n	n**ie**ce	c**i**ty	ch**ea**p

Write the words in the chart. Practice saying the words.

[fish icon]	[tree icon]
rich	________
________	________
________	________
________	________
________	________
________	________

More Words to Learn

Write translations and try to remember the words.

Word	Pronunciation	Translation
<u>sto</u>ry *noun*	/ˈstɔri/	
life (*pl.* lives) *noun*	/laɪf/	
<u>in</u>teresting *adjective*	/ˈɪntrəstɪŋ/	
im<u>po</u>ssible *adjective*	/ɪmˈpɑsəbl/	
die *verb*	/daɪ/	
sell *verb*	/sɛl/	
for<u>get</u> *verb*	/fərˈgɛt/	
stay *verb*	/steɪ/	
wi<u>thout</u> *preposition*	/wɪˈðaʊt/	
in the <u>end</u>	/ɪn ðə ɛnd/	

QUESTION TIME

Can you answer these questions?

1. Do you like romantic movies?
2. What's your favorite movie?
3. What do you think of horror movies?
4. What do you think of Tom Cruise?
5. What do you think of TV shows in your country?

Study Link MultiROM

Study Link www.oup.com/elt/americanenglishfile/1

I don't know anything about music.

Elvis Presley, American singer

Are you still mine?

1 VOCABULARY music

Complete the words.

1 I like listening to r*ock*________ music in my car.
2 Do you like going to k__________ bars?
3 Record companies don't like people who d__________ music from the Internet.
4 Michael plays the piano in a j__________ band.
5 It's very expensive to go to some pop c__________.
6 Why is Karl in that group? He can't s__________.
7 You need to learn to r__________ music before you can write it.
8 Kim doesn't like going to nightclubs, and she hates 1970s d__________ music.
9 When I listen to a song, I like to read the l__________.
10 My sister plays the violin in an o__________.
11 Which i__________ do you play? The cello.

2 GRAMMAR possessive pronouns

a Complete the questions and answers in the chart.

Whose…?	Possessive adjective	Possessive pronoun
Whose piano is that?	It's my piano.	*It's mine.*
Whose keys are those?	They're your keys.	*They're* _____.
__________?	It's his wallet.	__________.
__________?	They're her books.	__________.
__________?	It's our car.	__________.
__________?	They're your coats.	__________.
__________?	It's their house.	__________.

b Complete the sentences with a possessive adjective (*my*, *your*, etc.) or pronoun (*mine*, *yours*, etc.).

1 **Boy** Give it to me. It's *mine*.
Girl It's not _____. It's _____ dog! Give it to me.

2 It's not _____ cat. It's _____. _____ is black.

3 **Teacher** Whose is this? Is it _____, Jim?
Boy No, Sir. It's _____.
Girl Of course it's not _____. It's _____.

4 **A** Are these _____ coats?
B Yes, they're _____. Thanks very much.

Study Link **Student Book p.128** *Grammar Bank 4D*

3 PRONUNCIATION rhyming words

a Match the words that rhyme.

aunt see wear ~~wait~~ near eat hot water

1 hate	*wait*	5 daughter	__________
2 meet	__________	6 key	__________
3 hair	__________	7 not	__________
4 here	__________	8 can't	__________

b Practice saying the words.

4 READING

a Match the questions to the paragraphs.

What language? ~~When?~~ Why? Who? Where?

1 *When?*

The Eurovision Song Contest takes place in May every year. Before the final competition, people in each country choose the song they want to represent their country.

2 ____________________

The idea of the contest is to promote pop music from all of the different countries and to give an opportunity to new singers and composers.

3 ____________________

Only members of the European Broadcasting Union can participate in the competition. Singers don't have to have the nationality of the countries they represent. For example, in 1963 the singer Nana Mouskouri represented Luxembourg, although she is Greek. Since 1986, singers must be over 16, after a 13-year-old from Belgium won the competition the year before.

4 ____________________

In the first years of Eurovision, only the United Kingdom, Ireland, and Malta could sing in English. Now there are no rules about languages, so groups can sing in their own language or in English if they want to. Today almost all the contestants sing in English.

5 ____________________

The competition is always in the country where the last year's winner came from. The country with the most winners is Ireland, and many Eurovision singers have become very famous, for example Abba and Julio Iglesias.

b Guess the meaning of the highlighted words. Check your dictionary.

More Words to Learn

Write translations and try to remember the words.

Word	Pronunciation	Translation
head *noun*	/hɛd/	
group *noun*	/grup/	
lyrics *noun*	/ˈlɪrɪks/	
concert *noun*	/ˈkɑnsərt/	
similar *adjective*	/ˈsɪmələr/	
download *verb*	/ˈdaʊnloʊd/	
still *adverb*	/stɪl/	
tonight *adverb*	/təˈnaɪt/	
slowly *adverb*	/ˈsloʊli/	
What kind of...?	/wʌt kaɪnd əv/	

QUESTION TIME

Can you answer these questions?

1. What kind of music do you like?
2. Can you play the guitar?
3. Do you go to karaoke bars?
4. How often do you buy CDs?
5. Where do you like listening to music?

Study Link MultiROM

CAN YOU REMEMBER...? FILES 3&4

Complete each sentence with one word.

1. The children __________ cereal for breakfast.
2. He __________ eats meat. He's a vegetarian.
3. Is your birthday __________ the summer?
4. Kim comes from a __________ family. His father has a Rolls-Royce.
5. Jim's a good musician. He __________ play six instruments.
6. I hate __________ up early in the morning.
7. Tim loves Rebecca, but she doesn't love __________.
8. **A** Is this pen yours? **B** Yes, it's __________.

Study Link www.oup.com/elt/americanenglishfile/1

4 In a clothing store

1 VOCABULARY clothes

Write the words.

1 *a shirt*

2 p________

3 s________

4 a j________

5 j________

6 a s________

2 BUYING CLOTHES

Order the words to make questions.

A Can I help you?

B Yes / size / this / is / what / sweater

1 *Yes, what size is this sweater?*

A Let's see. It's a medium.

B a / have / you / small / Do

2 ________________?

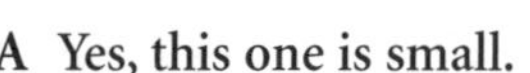

A Yes, this one is small.

B Thanks. on / can / it / I / Where / try

3 Thanks. ________________?

A The fitting rooms are over there.

B It fits. it / How / is / much

4 It fits. ________________?

A It's $59.99.

B credit cards / take / Do / you

5 ________________?

A Yes, of course.

3 SOCIAL ENGLISH

Complete the dialogue with one word in each blank.

A It's my birthday today.

B Oh! 1 *Happy* Birthday!

A 2 W________ you like to have dinner with me tonight?

B I'm sorry, I can't… I'm 3 b________ tonight.

A Oh. That's too bad. 4 H________ about Friday night?

B Yes, great.

A There's a new Vietnamese restaurant downtown. We can go there if you want.

B That's a good 5 i________.

4 READING

a Read the text.

SHOPPING IN TOKYO

1 Tokyo is a great place to shop for clothing and for electronics. Ginza is the best area for exclusive designer clothing. Akihabara is a good area for computers, phones, and cameras. The Nakamise Shopping Arcade is a great place to buy traditional souvenirs.

2 There are usually big sales in July and December in Tokyo. The most popular sales are for designer clothes, but that is not all that's on sale. You can find toys, food, electronics, and even wedding kimonos on sale!

3 Stores open between 10:00 and 11:00 a.m., and they close between 7:00 and 8:00 p.m. Most of the stores are also open on weekends and holidays.

4 You can't leave Tokyo without going to one of its many flea markets. You don't have to buy anything because it's fun just to look at the variety of things for sale. You can also go to the 100-yen stores. You can find chopsticks, fans, kites, and paper for $1.

b Match the questions below to paragraphs 1–4.

A Where can you buy cheap souvenirs? [*4*]

B When are Tokyo's stores open? [ ]

C When are the sales? [ ]

D Where are the main shopping areas in Tokyo? [ ]

My life is a simple thing that would interest nobody. It is a known fact that I was born, and that is all that is necessary.

Albert Einstein, German scientist

Who were they?

1 GRAMMAR *was / were*

a Complete the sentences with *was, were, wasn't,* or *weren't.*

A Who's that?

B It's William Shakespeare.

A Why [1] *was* he famous?

B He [2] ______ a writer.

A [3] ______ he Scottish?

B No, he [4] ______. He [5] ______ English. He [6] ______ born in Stratford-upon-Avon.

A And [7] ______ he married?

B Yes, he [8] ______. His wife's name [9] ______ Anne.

A And [10] ______ they happy?

B I don't know.

b Write questions and answers.

1 Mozart / from / Germany? ✗
Was Mozart from Germany?
No, he wasn't.

2 Columbus and Magellan / explorers? ✓
Were Columbus and Magellan explorers?
Yes, they were.

3 Virginia Woolf / writer? ✓
______________________?
______________.

4 the Beatles / from the US? ✗
______________________?
______________.

5 John McEnroe / soccer player? ✗
______________________?
______________.

6 Matisse / composer? ✗
______________________?
______________.

7 Picasso / born / Spain? ✓
______________________?
______________.

8 Greta Garbo / actress? ✓
______________________?
______________.

9 Tolstoy and Cervantes / painters? ✗
______________________?
______________.

10 Nelson Mandela / born / Brazil? ✗
______________________?
______________.

c Complete with present or past forms of *be.*

1 Today *is* Monday, so yesterday *was* Sunday.

2 **A** Hi. ______ your sister at home?
B No, she ______. She ______ here this morning, but now she ______ at work.

3 My books ______ here on my desk this morning. Where ______ they now?

4 Jon ______ born in Canada, but his parents ______ born in Singapore.

5 My boss ______ angry today because I ______ very late for work yesterday.

Study Link **Student Book p.130** *Grammar Bank 5A*

2 VOCABULARY word formation

a Make nouns from these words.

1 invent *an inventor*
2 write ______
3 politics ______
4 compose ______
5 music ______
6 paint ______
7 lead ______
8 act ______
9 science ______
10 dance ______

b Underline the stressed syllables, e.g., *an inventor.*

c Practice saying the words in **a**.

d Complete the sentences with *was / were* and a noun from **a**.

1 Galileo *was a scientist*.
2 The Wright brothers *were inventors*.
3 Frida Kahlo ______.
4 Gustav Mahler ______.
5 Jimi Hendrix ______.
6 The Brontë sisters ______.
7 Gandhi ______.
8 Fred Astaire ______.
9 Gregory Peck and Clark Gable ______.

More Words to Learn

Write translations and try to remember the words.

Word	Pronunciation	Translation
world *noun*	/wərld/	
statue *noun*	/ˈstætʃu/	
soldier *noun*	/ˈsoʊldʒər/	
war *noun*	/wɔr/	
battle *noun*	/ˈbætl/	
village *noun*	/ˈvɪlɪdʒ/	
great (= important) *adjective*	/greɪt/	
already *adverb*	/ɔlˈrɛdi/	
against *preposition*	/əˈgɛnst/	
(on the) left (*opposite* right)	/lɛft/	

Study idea

Try to remember words with other words or phrases:

1 remember words with their opposites, e.g., *left / right*
2 remember words in phrases, e.g., *on the left*

QUESTION TIME

Can you answer these questions?

1 Where were you born?
2 Where were your parents born?
3 Were you at home at 6 o'clock yesterday?
4 Who were you with?
5 How old were you on your last birthday?

Study Link MultiROM

To travel is to discover that everyone is wrong about other countries.
Aldous Huxley, British writer

Sydney, here we come!

1 PRONUNCIATION *-ed* endings

a Underline the word where *-ed* is pronounced /ɪd/.

1 booked	checked	wanted	walked
2 painted	arrived	turned	traveled
3 asked	waited	looked	worked
4 called	played	landed	listened
5 danced	watched	helped	started
6 worked	decided	followed	lived

b Practice saying the words.

2 GRAMMAR simple past: regular verbs

a Complete the sentences with a verb, first in the affirmative and then in the negative.

book show help ~~walk~~ play
paint study work

1 Yesterday Sam *walked* to work, but he *didn't walk* home.

2 I __________ Chinese at school, but I __________ German and Spanish.

3 The teacher __________ me with the exercise, but she __________ my friend.

4 Bill __________ basketball when he was young, but he __________ soccer.

5 They __________ the tickets but they __________ a hotel.

6 We __________ the living room, but we __________ the bedroom.

7 The salesperson __________ last Saturday, but she __________ on Sunday.

8 I __________ the photos to my sister, but I __________ them to my brother.

b Order the words to make questions.

1 after / Peter / match / tired / Was / the
A *Was Peter tired after the match?*
B Yes, he was.

2 you / night / Where / last / were
A __________________________?
B I was at home.

3 they / concert / late / the / Were / for
A __________________________?
B No, they weren't.

4 did / land / the / Where / plane
A __________________________?
B At the airport.

5 did / college / your / in / brother / What / study
A __________________________?
B Biology.

6 Was / tall / boyfriend / very / your / first
A __________________________?
B No, not really.

7 didn't / the / you / wait / Why / for / bus
A __________________________?
B Because it was too cold.

8 time / work / did / What / arrive / Sandra / yesterday / at
A __________________________?
B At ten o'clock.

c Complete the questions and answers.

Twentieth century quiz

1975 1985 ~~1929~~ 2001 1969 1925 1945

1 **when / Wall Street Crash / happen**
When did the Wall Street Crash happen?
It happened in 1929.

2 **when / the Second World War / end**
______________________________?
It ended in ________.

3 **when / Neil Armstrong / land / on the moon**
______________________________?
He landed on the moon in ________.

4 **when / cell phones / first / appear**
______________________________?
They first appeared in ________.

5 **when / John Logie Baird / invent the television**
______________________________?
He invented the television in ________.

6 **when / George Harrison / die**
______________________________?
He died in ________.

7 **when / Bill Gates / start Microsoft**
______________________________?
He started Microsoft in ________.

Study Link **Student Book p.130** *Grammar Bank 5B*

3 VOCABULARY past time expressions

Circle the correct answer.

1 She wasn't here (**last night**) / **yesterday night**.
2 My son was born **ago two years / two years ago**.
3 They traveled to the US **last month / the last month**.
4 Did you call me **last morning / yesterday morning**?
5 The plane landed **two hours ago / two ago hours**.
6 Mark arrived in Taipei **the last July / last July**.
7 I stayed with him **before two weeks / two weeks ago**.
8 Isabella booked the tickets **yesterday afternoon / last afternoon**.

More Words to Learn

Write translations and try to remember the words.

Word	Pronunciation	Translation
teenager *noun*	/ˈtineɪdʒər/	
trip *noun*	/trɪp/	
flight *noun*	/flaɪt/	
lucky *adjective*	/ˈlʌki/	
worried *adjective*	/ˈwərid/	
book (a ticket) *verb*	/bʊk/	
show *verb*	/ʃoʊ/	
arrive *verb*	/əˈraɪv/	
land *verb*	/lænd/	
so *conjunction*	/soʊ/	

QUESTION TIME

Can you answer these questions?

1 Did you study English yesterday?
2 Did you watch TV last night?
3 Did you travel by plane last year?
4 Did you cook dinner yesterday?
5 Did you start learning English a year ago?

Study Link **MultiROM**

Girls just want to have fun.
Cyndi Lauper, American singer

Girls' night out

1 VOCABULARY *go, have, get*

a Cross out the wrong expression.

1 GO to the beach out swimming ~~a bus~~
2 HAVE lunch a sandwich for a walk a drink
3 GET dressed a good time up a letter
4 GO to bed a taxi away to school
5 HAVE breakfast a drink a good time 18 years
6 GET shopping home a newspaper a taxi

b Fill in the blanks in the story with *went*, *had*, or *got*.

Last month Jane, a journalist from New York, 1 *went* to the Hamptons for the weekend. She booked a hotel on the Internet, and on Friday she 2 ______ the bus to the coast. It was very late when she arrived, so she just 3 ______ a ham and cheese sandwich and 4 ______ to bed. The next morning she 5 ______ up early and looked out of the window – it was raining! She took a shower and 6 ______ dressed. Then she 7 ______ out to buy a newspaper. Another hotel guest 8 ______ an umbrella and asked her if she needed it. They 9 ______ to the newsstand together, and after that they 10 ______ breakfast in a cafe. From then on, Jane didn't think about the rain – she 11 ______ a very good time in the Hamptons!

Study Link **Student Book p.150** *Vocabulary Bank*

2 GRAMMAR simple past irregular verbs

a Write sentences in the past.

1 Robert wears a tie to work. (yesterday)
Robert wore a tie to work yesterday.
2 They do their homework together. (last night)
______.
3 Helen doesn't go shopping. (last week)
______.
4 We meet in the restaurant. (last night)
______.
5 We don't have dinner at home. (last night)
______.
6 Jane gets up early. (yesterday morning)
______.
7 He buys a newspaper at the station. (yesterday)
______.
8 I leave home at 7:00. (yesterday)
______.
9 She sees her friends after work. (last night)
______.
10 Bob can't come to dinner. (last week)
______.

b Complete the questions in the dialogue.

A Where 1 *did you go* last night?
B I went to that new jazz club in town.
A 2 ______ good?
B Yes, it was great.
A Who 3 ______ with?
B I went with my boyfriend and some friends.
A What 4 ______?
B I wore my long jean skirt and a new top I bought last week.
A What time 5 ______ home?

B We got home at about 3:00 in the morning.

A 6_____________ a taxi home?

B No, my boyfriend has a car.

A Did 7_____________ a good time?

B Yes, we had a really great time. You can come with us next time, if you like.

A It depends. 8_____________ the jazz club expensive?

B No, not really.

Study Link **Student Book p.130** *Grammar Bank 5C*

3 READING

a Read the story.

THE WRONG BUS

A Japanese businessman had a big surprise last Sunday when he got the wrong bus to the airport and missed his flight.

Zenko Kajiyama, 32, went to Waverley station in Edinburgh, Scotland, to catch the bus to the airport. He had a meeting the next day in London, and he wanted to catch the evening flight. When he saw a silver bus marked Club Class he got on it. Unfortunately the bus was for people going to a birthday party.

The people on the bus helped Mr. Kajiyama with his bags and found him a seat. He thought he was on the right bus until they stopped at a bar and everyone got off. They asked Mr. Kajiyama to join their party and so he followed them into the bar. When he looked at his watch he saw it was too late and that he had missed his plane. At first he was very worried, but then he decided to stay in the bar. He had a drink and danced to the music with the other members of the party. In the end, he went back to the house of one of his new friends, and he slept on the sofa. The next morning he took a taxi to the airport and flew to London, but he was too late for his meeting.

Adapted from a website

b Mark the sentences T (true) or F (false).

1 Mr. Kajiyama wanted to catch the bus to London. *F*

2 He wanted to go to a party in London. ___

3 The Club Class bus didn't go to the airport. ___

4 Mr. Kajiyama went to the bar. ___

5 He didn't catch his plane. ___

6 In the end, he enjoyed the party. ___

7 He slept in the airport. ___

8 He didn't go to his meeting in London. ___

4 PRONUNCIATION simple past: irregular verbs

a Circle the word with a different vowel sound.

æ	ɑ	ɔ	eɪ	ɛ
swam	cost	bought	ate	met
(came)	wrote	saw	made	left
sang	got	heard	said	fell
sat	hot	called	paid	knew

b Practice saying the words.

More Words to Learn

Write translations and try to remember the words.

Word	Pronunciation	Translation
makeup *noun*	/ˈmeɪkʌp/	
pie *noun*	/paɪ/	
wine *noun*	/waɪn/	
dress *noun*	/drɛs/	
fashions *noun*	/ˈfæʃnz/	
literature *noun*	/ˈlɪtərətʃər/	
great (= fantastic) *adjective*	/greɪt/	
open / closed *adjectives*	/ˈoʊpən/ /kloʊzd/	
pay for *verb*	/ˈpeɪ fər/	
especially *adverb*	/ɪˈspɛʃəli/	

QUESTION TIME

Can you answer these questions?

1 Did you go out last Saturday?

2 What did you do?

3 Did you have a good time?

4 What did you have for dinner last night?

5 What did you wear yesterday?

Study Link **MultiROM**

Elementary, my dear Watson.
Attributed to Sherlock Holmes (but he never said it)

Murder in a mansion

1 PRONUNCIATION simple past verbs

a Match the verbs with the same vowel sound.

drove could ~~made~~ said learned bought had lost

1 came	*made*	5 saw	______
2 left	______	6 spoke	______
3 taught	______	7 took	______
4 ran	______	8 heard	______

b Practice saying the words.

2 VOCABULARY irregular verbs

a Complete the base form and past forms of these irregular verbs. Use *a, e, i, o,* or *u*.

Base form	Past	Base form	Past
beg*i*n	beg*a*n	p_t	p_t
c_me	c_me	r_ng	r_ng
dr_nk	dr_nk	s_t	s_t
dr_ve	dr_ve	w_ke up	w_ke up
g_ve	g_ve	w_n	w_n
kn_w	kn_w	wr_te	wr_te

b Complete the sentences with the simple past form of the verbs in the box.

buy find ~~hear~~ make ~~get~~ not take
can't go lose meet think

1 He *got* up in the middle of the night because he *heard* a noise.
2 I ______ Sally at a party last week.
3 They ______ a new car two days ago.
4 We ______ to bed very late last night.
5 Karen ______ dinner yesterday. It was pasta, as usual.
6 She was sick, so she ______ her dog for a walk this morning.
7 When we arrived in Paris, we ______ a cheap hotel near the station.
8 The game was a disaster. Our team ______.
9 I ______ she was Italian, but she was Spanish.
10 I looked everywhere, but I ______ find my glasses.

Study Link **Student Book p.154** *Irregular verbs*

3 GRAMMAR simple past

a Read this police report. Complete the sentences with the simple past form of the verbs in the box.

be (x2) ~~arrive~~ leave not want see can't
go not run look open find take

Police report: bank robbery

We [1] *arrived* at the bank at 9:36 in the evening, and we [2] ______ our police car outside. The bank [3] ______ closed and all the lights [4] ______ off, but we [5] ______ through the window. We [6] ______ a person inside the bank. At first we [7] ______ see who it was, but then he [8] ______ the door and came out – it was Steven Potter. He [9] ______ away – he just walked slowly to his car. Then he drove away. The next morning, we [10] ______ to his house at 6:00 a.m. We [11] ______ him in bed. He [12] ______ to speak to us, so we [13] ______ him to the police station.

b Complete the questions with the correct form of the verbs in parentheses.

POLICE OFFICER Where [1] *were you* at about 9:30 yesterday evening? (be)

STEVEN POTTER I was at a movie. It started at 9:00.

PO What movie [2] ________ ? (see)

SP I can't remember. It wasn't very good.

PO Hmm. Very interesting. And who [3] ________ to the movie with? (go)

SP My girlfriend.

PO [4] ________ the movie? (like)

SP Yes, she thought it was very good.

PO What time [5] ________ the movie ________? (end)

SP At about 10:30.

PO And what [6] ________ after you left the movie? (do)

SP We went to a restaurant – *La Dolce Vita*, on State Street.

PO *La Dolce Vita*? I know it. Very good spaghetti. What time [7] ________ the restaurant? (leave)

SP At about 12:00.

PO That's very late. [8] ________ home after that? (go)

SP No, we went to a nightclub – *Flanagan's*. Then we went home.

PO How? [9] ________ a taxi? (take)

SP No, we took a bus.

PO And what time [10] ________ to bed? (go)

SP At about 4:00 a.m. Can I go home now? I'm tired.

PO No, I'd like to ask you some more questions…

More Words to Learn

Write translations and try to remember the words.

Word	Pronunciation	Translation
mansion *noun*	/ˈmænʃn/	
millionaire *noun*	/mɪlyəˈnɛr/	
library *noun*	/ˈlaɪbrɛri/	
murder *noun*	/ˈmərdər/	
asleep *adjective*	/əˈslip/	
dead *adjective*	/dɛd/	
happen *verb*	/ˈhæpən/	
everybody *pronoun*	/ˈɛvribʌdi/	
somebody *pronoun*	/ˈsʌmbʌdi/	
nobody *pronoun*	/ˈnoʊbʌdi/	

QUESTION TIME

Can you answer these questions?

1 What time did you get up yesterday?
2 Where were you at two o'clock?
3 Where did you go after lunch?
4 Did you go out in the evening?
5 What time did you go to bed?

Study Link MultiROM

CAN YOU REMEMBER…? FILES 4&5

Complete each sentence with one word.

1 **A** ________ your daughter swim?
B Yes, but not very well.
2 Do you like ________ to the gym?
3 We help them and they help ________.
4 **A** Whose car is this?
B It's ________. We bought it last week.
5 Where ________ you born?
6 I ________ go out last night. I was very tired.
7 Did you ________ a good time at the party?
8 We ________ to a really good restaurant last night.

5 In a gift shop

1 VOCABULARY shopping

Write the words.

1 p*ostcards* 3 a m______ 5 b______

2 a m______ 4 T-______

2 BUYING A PRESENT

Order the dialogue.

- A Next, please. [1]
- B No, thanks. Just the mug. [ ]
- A It's $5. [ ]
- B How much is a large mug? [ ]
- A These mugs are very cheap. [ ]
- B How much are the T-shirts? [2]
- B Red, please. [ ]
- A Red or blue? [ ]
- B Oh! They're very expensive! [ ]
- A Here you are. Anything else? [ ]
- A They're $30. [ ]
- B OK. Can I have a mug, please? [ ]

3 SOCIAL ENGLISH

Complete the dialogue with these words.

believe Come look nice problem Relax time ~~Wow~~

A Hi, Sally. [1] *Wow*! You [2]______ great. Nice dress!

B Here's a little present for you.

A That's very [3]______ of you. Oh no, it's broken.

B I don't [4]______ it! I'm sorry, Carl.

A No [5]______. What time did you make the reservation for?

B For 8 o'clock. [6]______ on. It's [7]______ to go. It's late.

A [8]______, Sally. We have time. We can get a taxi.

4 READING

a Complete the text with these words.

cookies love cup ~~shops~~ find popular

Souvenirs from Mexico

What do visitors to Mexico take home as a souvenir? We visited a lot of souvenir [1] *shops* in Mexico City, and this is what we found.

Hot chocolate

Mexicans love their hot chocolate, and tourists seem to love it, too. You can buy it in bars and powder, and mix it with milk at home. And why not buy a hand-painted [2]______ or a mug at the same time? And to have with your hot chocolate, what about some Mexican [3]______ or some traditional bread or candy?

Postcards and pictures

Postcards and pictures of famous sights are very [4]______ souvenirs. The Floating Gardens? The pyramids? You can [5]______ all these and a lot of other places, too! Tourists also buy postcards or copies of paintings by Frida Kahlo or Diego Rivera.

Other souvenirs

People also [5]______ shopping in the Zona Rosa. Souvenir shops are full of mugs, postcards, T-shirts, silver jewelry, and pottery.

b Underline five words or phrases you don't know. Use your dictionary to look up their meaning and pronunciation.

If you want breakfast in bed, sleep in the kitchen.
Allison Pearson, British writer

A house with a history

1 VOCABULARY apartments and houses

a Write the room.

office ~~hall~~ dining room
bedroom living room kitchen
garage bathroom

Where do you usually…

1 … take off your coat? In the *hall*.
2 … take a shower? In the ______.
3 … have dinner? In the ______.
4 … use a computer? In the ______.
5 … park your car? In the ______.
6 … make lunch? In the ______.
7 … watch television? In the ______.
8 … sleep? In the ______.

b Complete the crossword.

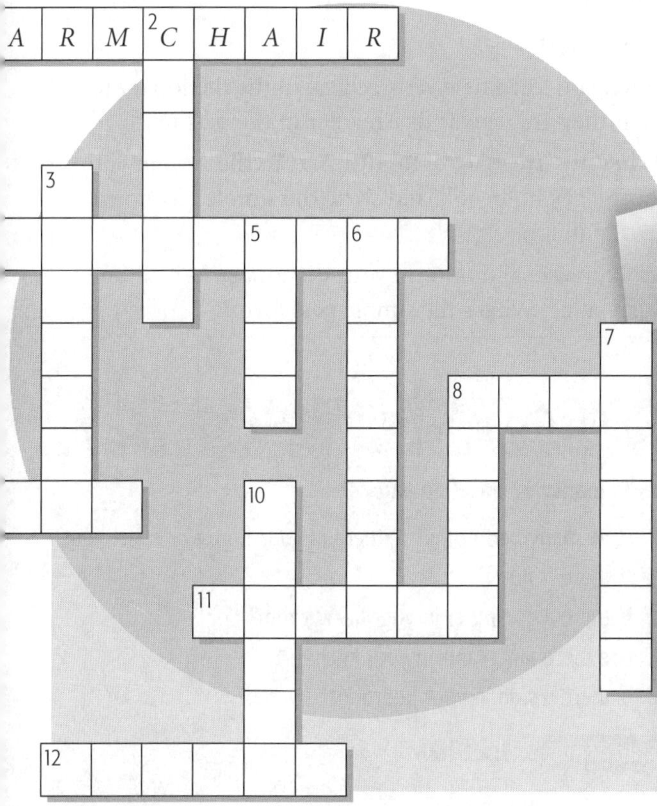

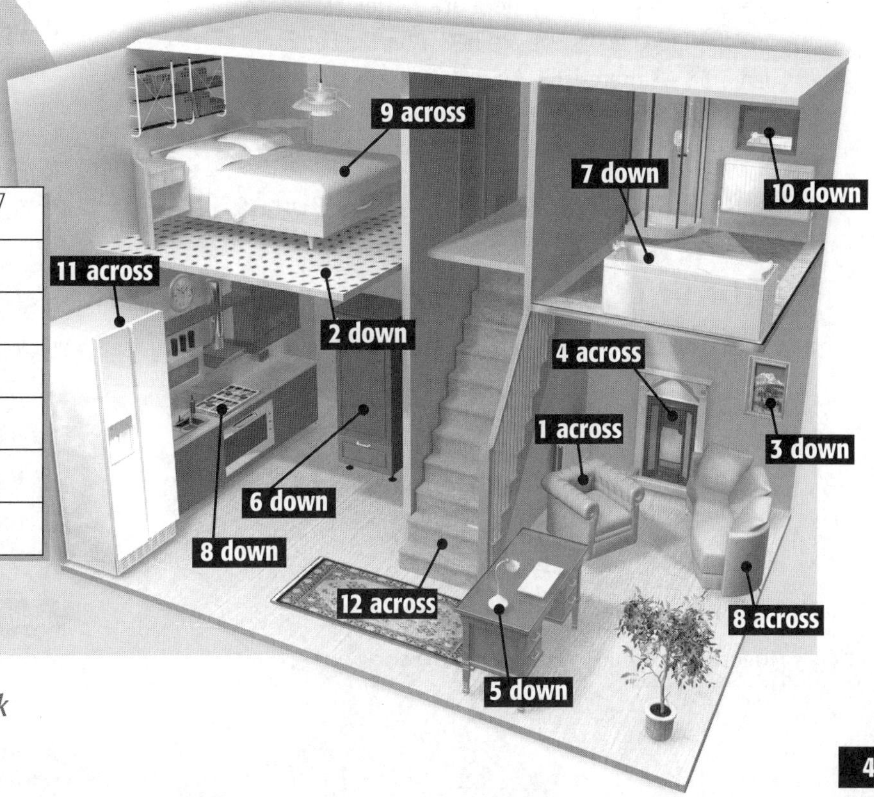

1 *A R M* 2 *C H A I R*

3, 5, 6, 7, 8, 10, 11, 12

9 across, 7 down, 10 down, 11 across, 2 down, 4 across, 1 across, 3 down, 6 down, 8 down, 12 across, 8 across, 5 down

2 GRAMMAR *there is / there are*

a Complete with the correct form of *there is / there are* and, if necessary, *a*, *some*, or *any*.

A Could you give me some more information about the house?
B Of course. What do you want to know?
A 1 *Is there a* yard?
B Yes, 2 ______ large yard, with a swimming pool.
A Oh, very nice! And how many bedrooms 3 ______?
B Three, I think…yes, 4 ______ three bedrooms.
A And 5 ______ dining room?
B No, 6 ______. But 7 ______ big kitchen.
A 8 ______ shelves in the kitchen?
B No, 9 ______. But 10 ______ cupboards. Do you have any more questions?
A Yes. The furniture… 11 ______ armchairs in the living room?
B No, I'm sorry. 12 ______ armchairs, but 13 ______ sofa.

Study Link Student Book p.151 *Vocabulary Bank*

b Write the sentences in the plural.

1 There's a towel on the floor.

There are some towels on the floor.

2 Is there a plant in your living room?

_______________________________________?

3 There's a key in that door.

_______________________________________.

4 Is there a restroom in this restaurant?

_______________________________________?

5 There isn't a window in this room.

_______________________________________.

c Circle the correct form.

[1] (It's) / **There's** a very nice house. [2] **There's / It's** a large yard, and [3] **there are / they are** some trees in the yard. I think [4] **there are / they are** apple trees. [5] **There's / It's** a living room, with a big blue sofa. In the kitchen, [6] **there aren't / they aren't** any shelves, but [7] **there are / they are** some cupboards. [8] **There are / They are** very old, but the fridge and stove are new. And the bathroom's fantastic – [9] **there isn't / it isn't** very big, but [10] **there's / it's** a shower and a bathtub!

Study Link **Student Book p.132** *Grammar Bank 6A*

3 PRONUNCIATION /ð/ and /ɛr/, word stress

a Circle the word with a different sound.

ð	θ	ɛr	ɪr
bro**th**er	**th**irsty	here	engin**eer**
(**th**ink)	**th**ing	h**air**	w**ear**
then	**th**at	wh**ere**	n**ear**
toge**th**er	**th**anks	st**air**s	h**ere**

b Underline the stressed syllable. Which two words are not stressed on the first syllable?

1 carpet	4 fantastic	7 bedroom
2 mirror	5 fireplace	8 information
3 cupboard	6 sofa	

c Practice saying the words in **a** and **b**.

More Words to Learn

Write translations and try to remember the words.

Word	Pronunciation	Translation
price *noun*	/praɪs/	
paintings *noun*	/ˈpeɪntɪŋz/	
real estate agent *noun*	/ril ɪˈsteɪt ˈeɪdʒənt/	
plants *noun*	/plænts/	
large *adjective*	/ˈlɑrdʒ/	
quiet *adjective*	/ˈkwaɪət/	
local *adjective*	/ˈloʊkl/	
original *adjective*	/əˈrɪdʒənl/	
rent *verb*	/rɛnt/	
draw *verb*	/drɔ/	

Study idea

Irregular verbs

1 When you learn new verbs, check in the dictionary to see if they are regular or irregular in the past tense.

2 If they are irregular, write IRR next to the verb in your vocabulary notebook, and write the simple past form next to it, too.

3 Look up *rent* and *draw* in your dictionary. Which one is irregular? What's the simple past form?

QUESTION TIME

Can you answer these questions?

1 How many bedrooms are there in your house or apartment?
2 Is there a study?
3 Is there a computer in your living room?
4 Are there any plants in your kitchen?
5 Is there a sofa in your bedroom?

Study Link **MultiROM**

Study Link www.oup.com/elt/americanenglishfile/1

The past is a ghost, the future a dream, and all we ever have is now.
Bill Cosby, American comedian

A night in a haunted hotel

1 VOCABULARY prepositions of place

Complete the sentences with these words.

over	~~in~~	between	on	in front of
in	behind	next to	under	across from

1 There's a big table *in* the room.
2 There's a small table ________ the door.
3 There's a black dog ________ the table.
4 A cat is sitting ________ the fireplace.
5 There's a ghost sitting ________ the woman.
6 Another ghost is standing ________ the woman.
7 There are some glasses ________ the cupboard.
8 There are some plates ________ the table.
9 There's a picture ________ the fireplace.
10 There's a sofa ________ the two armchairs.

2 GRAMMAR *there was / there were*

a Complete the text. Use *was*, *were*, *wasn't*, or *weren't*.

I went on vacation to Greece last month. I stayed in a really nice hotel – there [1] *were* two swimming pools outside! There [2] ________ a small beach in front of the hotel. There [3] ________ any cars on the road, but there [4] ________ some buses and a lot of tourists. There [5] ________ a restaurant in the hotel, but there [6] ________ some very nice restaurants in the town. There [7] ________ a waiter named Manolis – he was very friendly. There [8] ________ a big window, so I could see the ocean. In the evening, when there [9] ________ any people on the beach, it was very beautiful.

b Complete the dialogue.

A Did you have a nice vacation in Greece?
B Yes, it was great. The hotel was really nice.
A Was it? [1] *Was* *there* a swimming pool?
B Yes, [2] ________ ________ two swimming pools.
A Two swimming pools! Wow! What about your room?
B [3] ________ ________ a big bed, but [4] ________ ________ a television. [5] ________ ________ a minibar and a beautiful sofa next to the window.
A [6] ________ ________ any other Canadian tourists?
B No, [7] ________ ________. But [8] ________ ________ some Italians and some Americans.
A [9] ________ ________ a restaurant in the hotel?
B No, [10] ________ ________. But [11] ________ ________ some nice restaurants in the town.

Study Link **Student Book p.132** *Grammar Bank 6B*

3 READING

a Read the advertisement.

Castle for rent

This beautiful 17th-century castle in southern France has 60 acres of land. The owners live in the east wing of the castle and rent the rest of the building to tourists.

In front of the main entrance to the castle there's a rose garden and a pretty fountain, which is lit up at night. In the garden there's a heated swimming pool with a wonderful terrace for sunbathing.

There's room in the castle for 20 people to sleep. There are 10 bedrooms on the first and second floors, all of which have a television, and there are six bathrooms. There's a large formal dining room on the first floor, where eight people can eat, and there's a dining area outside, where all 20 guests can have dinner together. For relaxing in the evening, there's a large living room with sofas and armchairs. Downstairs there's also a study and a very spacious kitchen with doors to the garden.

The house is cleaned twice a week and there is a babysitting service.

Adapted from a website

b Read the ad again and answer the questions.

1 How old is the castle?
2 Who lives in the castle?
3 What two things can you do in the garden?
4 How many bedrooms are there?
5 Where can 20 guests eat together?
6 How often do people come to clean the house?

c Guess the meaning of the highlighted words. Check your dictionary.

4 PRONUNCIATION silent letters

a Cross out the silent consonants.

1 g~~h~~ost	6 could
2 island	7 write
3 comb	8 half
4 listen	9 cupboard
5 white	10 hour

b Practice saying the words.

More Words to Learn

Write translations and try to remember the words.

Word	Pronunciation	Translation
ghost *noun*	/goʊst/	
century *noun*	/ˈsɛntʃəri/	
priest *noun*	/prist/	
guest *noun*	/gɛst/	
nervous *adjective*	/ˈnərvəs/	
frightened *adjective*	/ˈfraɪtnd/	
strange *adjective*	/streɪndʒ/	
believe *verb*	/bɪˈliv/	
go back *verb*	/goʊ bæk/	
spend (the night) *verb*	/spɛnd/	

QUESTION TIME

Can you answer these questions?

1 Where's the TV in your house or apartment?
2 What building is across from your school?
3 How many people were there in your last English class?
4 Was there a good movie on TV last night?
5 Was there a festival in your town last month?

Study Link MultiROM

Don't throw stones at your neighbors if your own windows are glass.
Benjamin Franklin, American politician

Nightmare neighbors

1 VOCABULARY verb phrases

Complete the text with the correct form of these verbs.

~~argue~~ move bark cry talk have watch play

My neighbors, Mr. and Mrs. Jackson, are terrible. They [1] *argue* all the time and their dog [2] ________ all day. They have a three-month-old baby who [3] ________ every night, and Mr. Jackson [4] ________ the violin early in the morning. Then Mrs. Jackson gets up, and they [5] ________ loudly about everything. In the evening, they often [6] ________ their furniture around and they [7] ________ TV late at night. And on weekends, they often [8] ________ noisy parties!

2 GRAMMAR present continuous

a Complete the dialogue.

A What [1] *are you doing* (you / do), Grandma?
B I [2] ________________ (look) at the neighbors.
A What [3] ________________ (they / do)?
[4] ________________ (Mrs. Jackson / watch) TV?
B No, she [5] ________________ (move) the furniture.
A And [6] ________________ (Mr. Jackson / play) the violin?
B Yes, he is. Oh, look! Some people [7] ________________ (arrive). I think they want to have a party. Mr. Jackson [8] ________________ (open) the door...

b Look at the picture of a park. What are the people doing?

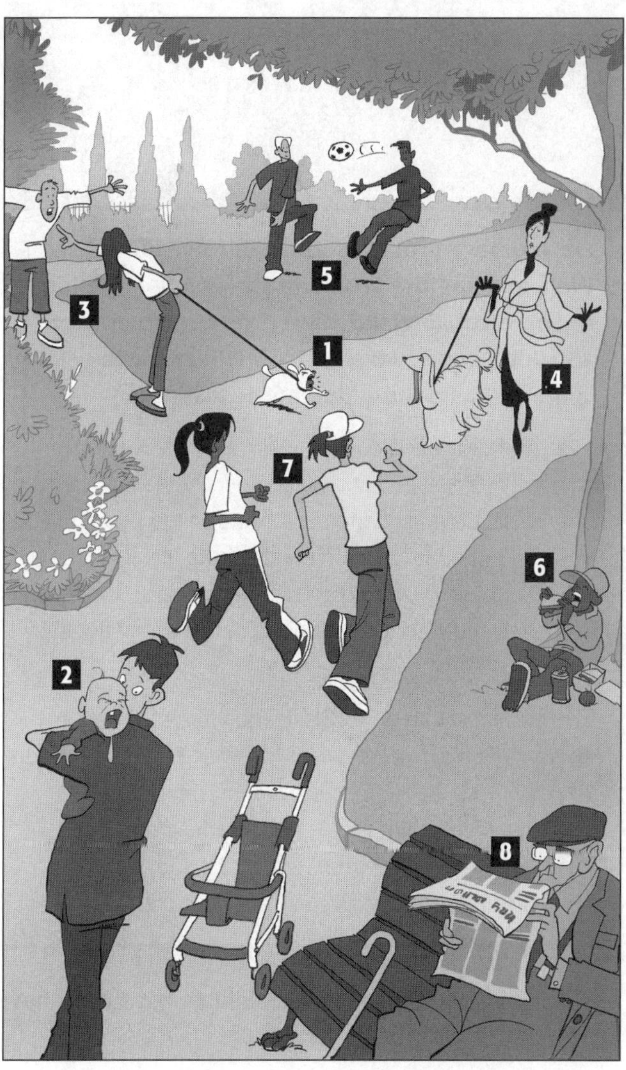

1 *The dog's barking.*
2 ________________________.
3 ________________________.
4 ________________________.
5 ________________________.
6 ________________________.
7 ________________________.
8 ________________________.

Study Link Student Book p.132 *Grammar Bank 6C*

3 READING

a Read the text.

Noisy neighbors

Do you have problems with your neighbors? Well, imagine the problems the people of Pilton in Somerset, England, have. Every summer over 150,000 people travel to their village for the annual Glastonbury pop music festival.

Every year, for three days, the village is full of people of all ages who leave cans and papers all over the streets. The music plays until the early hours of the morning and you can hear people talking and singing all night. The quiet country village becomes a nightmare to live in, and some residents are even thinking of moving to another village.

The pop fans who go to Glastonbury usually sleep in tents in a field, but last year Mr. James Findlay, a resident of Pilton, found two people asleep in his yard in the morning. Mr. Findlay said, "I don't want to stop the Glastonbury Festival. I just want the fans to enjoy the festival without disturbing normal village life."

b Check ☑ the problems the villagers of Pilton have with their temporary neighbors.

1 ☐ Their dogs bark.
2 ☐ They throw their trash on the street.
3 ☐ They listen to loud music.
4 ☐ Their babies cry all night.
5 ☐ They make a lot of noise.
6 ☐ They go into other people's yards.
7 ☐ They watch TV late at night.
8 ☐ They break things in the village.

c Guess the meaning of the highlighted words. Check your dictionary.

4 PRONUNCIATION verb + *-ing*

a Circle the word with a different sound.

ɪ	drinking	(writing)	swimming	giving
i	meeting	reading	speaking	hearing
ɔ	talking	walking	moving	calling
eɪ	playing	having	raining	painting
oʊ	knowing	going	doing	closing
aɪ	living	buying	finding	riding

b Practice saying the words.

More Words to Learn

Write translations and try to remember the words.

Word	Pronunciation	Translation
neighbor *noun*	/ˈneɪbər/	
violin *noun*	/vaɪəˈlɪn/	
baby *noun*	/ˈbeɪbi/	
noisy *adjective*	/ˈnɔɪzi/	
friendly *adjective*	/ˈfrɛndli/	
choose *verb*	/tʃuz/	
argue *verb*	/ˈɑrgyu/	
cry *verb*	/kraɪ/	
bark *verb*	/bɑrk/	
move *verb*	/muv/	

QUESTION TIME

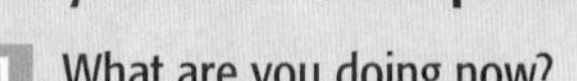

Can you answer these questions?

1 What are you doing now?
2 Are you listening to music?
3 What are your parents doing?
4 Are you doing this exercise at home?
5 Do you have noisy neighbors?

Study Link **MultiROM**

I want to wake up in the city that never sleeps.
Fred Ebb, American songwriter

New York, New York

1 GRAMMAR simple present or present continuous?

a Circle the correct form.

1 **A** **What do you do** / **What are you doing** here?
B I'm waiting for a friend.

2 **Do you walk** / **Are you walking** to work every day?

3 Barbara isn't here. She **buys** / **'s buying** a present for her daughter.

4 I **go** / **'m going** to work now. See you later.

5 It **rains** / **'s raining** a lot here in the winter.

6 **A** Where's Laura?
B She's on the phone. She**'s talking** / **talks** to Paul.

7 **Does your baby cry** / **Is your baby crying** at night?

8 My husband **watches** / **'s watching** soccer three times a week.

b Complete the sentences. Use the simple present or present continuous.

1 What time *does he start* (he / start) work every day?

2 David's in the bathroom. He ________ (take) a shower.

3 **A** Where's Sally?
B She ________ (do) her homework.

4 Peter and Clare ________ (not / like) their neighbors.

5 My parents ________ (look) for a new house right now.

6 Lisa usually ________ (cook) dinner during the week.

7 I ________ (watch) a show on TV. Can you call me later?

8 My husband ________ (go) to bed very late – usually at midnight.

9 We ________ (not / want) to drive to Florida. It's too far away!

10 **A** Where ________ (you / go)?
B To the bank. See you later.

Study Link **Student Book p.132** *Grammar Bank 6D*

2 VOCABULARY town and city

a Complete the sentences with a word from each box.

police ~~art~~ department sports shopping train travel

center station store agency station mall ~~gallery~~

1 Where can you see paintings?
In an *art* *gallery*.

2 Where can you visit different stores?
At a ________ ________.

3 Where can you get a train?
At a ________ ________.

4 Where can you book a vacation?
At a ________ ________.

5 Where can you talk to a police officer?
At a ________ ________.

6 Where can you buy clothes for all of the family?
In a ________ ________.

7 Where can you play basketball?
At a ________ ________.

b Complete the puzzle.

Study Link **Student Book p.152** *Vocabulary Bank*

3 PRONUNCIATION /ə/

a Underline the /ə/ sound.

1 museum	6 ago
2 palace	7 refrigerator
3 carpet	8 garage
4 sofa	9 tomorrow
5 kitchen	10 parent

b Practice saying the words.

More Words to Learn

Write translations and try to remember the words.

Word	Pronunciation	Translation
ship *noun*	/ʃɪp/	
line *noun*	/laɪn/	
trip *noun*	/trɪp/	
passenger *noun*	/ˈpæsəndʒər/	
building *noun*	/ˈbɪldɪŋ/	
view *noun*	/vyu/	
subway *noun*	/ˈsʌbweɪ/	
around *preposition*	/əˈraʊnd/	
busy *adjective*	/ˈbɪzi/	
That's too bad!	/ðætz tu bæd/	

QUESTION TIME

Can you answer these questions?

1 What kind of books do you read?
2 What are you reading now?
3 What do you usually wear?
4 What are you wearing now?
5 What's the main tourist attraction in your town?

Study Link **MultiROM**

CAN YOU REMEMBER...? FILES 5&6

Complete each sentence with one word.

1 My grandparents ________ doctors. They died before I was born.
2 ________ they book their vacation on the Internet last summer?
3 We ________ pizza and sodas for lunch yesterday.
4 I ________ see the end of the movie because I fell asleep.
5 There ________ two bathrooms in my new house.
6 There ________ many people at the beach yesterday – it was very cold.
7 Listen! The neighbors are ________ noise again.
8 **A** ________ you staying at a hotel or with friends?
B We're in a little hotel downtown.

Study Link www.oup.com/elt/americanenglishfile/1

1 VOCABULARY directions

Complete the words and phrases.

1 on the c*orner*______
2 at the t______ l______
3 a t______ c______
4 a______ f______
5 turn l______
6 turn r______
7 go s______ a______
8 go p______ the station

2 ASKING FOR DIRECTIONS

Complete the dialogue with these words.

exactly ~~Excuse~~ near say first tell way Where's

A [1] *Excuse* me. [2]______ Barton Street, please?
B Sorry, I don't know.
A Excuse me. Is Barton Street [3]______ here?
C Barton Street? I know the name, but I don't know [4]______ where it is. Sorry.
A Excuse me. Can you [5]______ me the [6]______ to Barton Street?
D Yes. Turn right at the traffic light. Then it's the [7]______ street on your left.
A Sorry, could you [8]______ that again?

3 SOCIAL ENGLISH

Match the phrases.

1 Let's ask that man. — b
2 You were right.
3 Excuse me. We're lost.
4 Don't be angry.

a I'm only joking.
b He probably knows the way.
c It was the house on the corner.
d Could you help us?

4 READING

a Read the information about getting around London.

Getting around New York City

By subway

The New York subway is enormous and can take you everywhere quickly. However, the stations are hot and uncomfortable in the summer, and the system can be confusing for tourists, who often get on the wrong train. It can also be very crowded during "rush hour" (7:00–9:00 in the morning and 5:00–7:00 in the evening).

By bus

The buses give you a good view of the sights, but if traffic is bad, your trip can take a long time. Before you take the subway or the bus, you should first buy a Metrocard. A Metrocard is a plastic card that people use on both buses and the subway in New York City.

By taxi or car

Taxis are great but expensive. Driving in New York, especially Manhattan, is not recommended – it's almost impossible to park, and New York drivers have a reputation for being aggressive.

b Answer the questions.

1 When is the subway usually very busy?
2 Where is a good place to sit to see the sights?
3 Where can you use Metrocards?
4 What is the problem with taking a taxi?
5 What is the reputation of New York drivers?

c Match the highlighted adjectives to their meanings.

very big *enormous*
very good ______
full of people ______
difficult to understand ______

If it tastes good, it's bad for you.
Isaac Asimov, science fiction writer

What does your food say about you?

1 VOCABULARY food

a Complete the crossword.

b Write the words in the correct column.

apples cake ~~carrots~~ pineapple
onions grapes chocolate mushrooms
peas potato chips bananas cookies

Vegetables	Snacks	Fruit
carrots		

Study Link **Student Book p.153** *Vocabulary Bank*

2 GRAMMAR *a / an, some / any*

a What did Mark and Jan buy when they went shopping yesterday? Write *a*, *an*, or *some* in the spaces.

1 some meat
2 ______ apple
3 ______ cheese
4 ______ milk
5 ______ butter
6 ______ banana
7 ______ pineapple
8 ______ oranges
9 ______ onion
10 ______ tomatoes

b Write the sentences in the affirmative or negative.

1 There's some rice in the cupboard.
There isn't any rice in the cupboard.

2 I ______________________.
I didn't eat any fruit yesterday.

3 I ______________________.
I didn't have an egg for breakfast.

4 There ______________________.
There isn't any sugar in this coffee.

5 We have some vegetables in the garden.
We ______________________.

6 There ______________________.
There weren't any sandwiches in the fridge.

7 There was some good fish at the supermarket.
There ______________________.

8 I had a salad for lunch.
I ______________________.

c Complete the dialogue with *a*, *an*, *some*, or *any*.

A I'm going to the supermarket. Would you like anything?

B Yes, can you get [1] *some* milk and [2] ______ bottle of water?

A But there's [3] ______ milk in the fridge.

B No, there isn't. I drank it this morning. And we need 4______ bread for sandwiches tomorrow. Oh, yes – do we have 5______ cheese? I'd like to make 6______ pizza this evening.

A Yes, I think there's 7______ cheese in the fridge. And there are 8______ tomatoes, too.

B And I'd like 9______ onion too, please. I don't think we have 10______ . Oh, and we need 11______ eggs…

Study Link **Student Book p.134** *Grammar Bank 7A*

3 PRONUNCIATION the letters *ea*

Circle the word with a different sound. Practice saying the words.

ɪ	meat	breakfast	tea
ɛ	bread	healthy	ice cream
eɪ	eat	great	steak

4 READING

a Match each "food fact" to the paragraph which explains why it's false.

A Eating too much sugar can make you addicted. ☐

B Beer is good for your hair. ☐

C Eating fruit at the end of a meal is very healthy. ☐

D Putting salt in water will make it boil faster. *1*

Food facts...or are they?

1 Many cooks always put salt into water before putting in the pasta. Many say that this helps the water boil more quickly, but this isn't true. In fact, salt makes water boil at a higher temperature, so the water boils more slowly.

2 Putting beer on your hair is not a good idea. The only result is a shower that smells like a bar and hair that looks terrible. It is impossible for the beer to make your hair more beautiful, believe me, so don't try it.

3 When people eat a lot of sweet things, it isn't because their body really needs sugar. It's because they like the taste, and they often have a lot of sweet things like cakes and cookies in their cupboards. Sugar is not a drug and eating it is just a bad habit.

4 Fruit is quite difficult to digest. If you eat it at the end of a meal, it can stay in your stomach for a long time. This means that you can feel very uncomfortable if you've just eaten a very big meal. The best time to eat fruit is between meals.

b Guess the meaning of the highlighted words. Check your dictionary.

More Words to Learn

Write translations and try to remember the words.

Word	Pronunciation	Translation
(shopping) basket *noun*	/ˈbæskət/	
spaghetti *noun*	/spəˈgɛti/	
dish *noun*	/dɪʃ/	
ingredients *noun*	/ɪnˈgridiənts/	
luxury *noun*	/ˈlʌkʃəri/	
missing *adjective*	/ˈmɪsɪŋ/	
countable *adjective*	/ˈkaʊntəbl/	
uncountable *adjective*	/ʌnˈkaʊntəbl/	

Study idea

1 Try to connect new words with other words in English or in your language, e.g., shopping **basket** – **basket**ball.

2 Look at the words in **More Words to Learn**. Can you connect them to any other words?

QUESTION TIME

Can you answer these questions?

1 What do you usually have for breakfast?

2 What do you drink with your dinner?

3 What's your favorite food?

4 What vegetables don't you like?

5 What do you drink when you go out with your friends?

Study Link **MultiROM**

Human beings are 70% water. With some people, the rest is collagen.
Martin Mull, American actor and writer

How much water do we really need?

1 PRONUNCIATION /w/, /v/, and /b/

a William, Vera, and Brenda are thinking about the presents they want for their birthdays. William wants presents that begin with /w/, Vera wants those that begin with /v/, and Brenda wants those that begin with /b/. What presents do they each want?

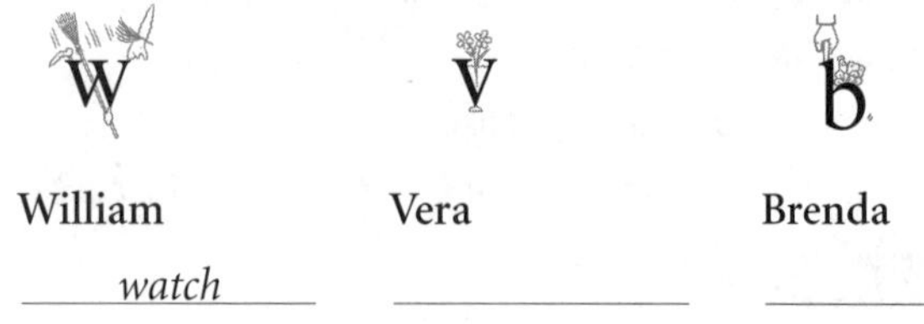

William	Vera	Brenda
watch	______	______
______	______	______

b Practice saying the words.

2 GRAMMAR *how much / how many?*, quantifiers

a Complete the questions. Then complete the sentences.

1 *He doesn't eat many cookies.*

2 He ______________________.

3 She ______________________.

4 He ______________________.

5 She ______________________.

6 She ______________________.

b Read about these records in competitive eating.

Competitive eating

	Alina Baden ate 46 hot dogs in 11 minutes.
	George Willis ate 128 chicken wings in 28 minutes.
	Nikolai Cohen ate 10 hamburgers in 11 minutes.
	John Edwards ate almost 2 gallons of ice cream in 14 minutes.
	Gustav Sajer drank 6 liters of milk in 3 minutes 29 seconds.
	Barbara Beard ate 11 pounds of fruit (bananas and apples) in 9 minutes 15 seconds.

Write questions.

1 *How many hamburgers did Nikolai Cohen eat?*
Ten.

2 ______________________________?
Six liters.

3 ______________________________?
Almost two gallons.

4 ______________________________?
A hundred and twenty-eight.

5 ______________________________?
Eleven pounds.

6 ______________________________?
Forty-six.

Study Link **Student Book p.134** *Grammar Bank 7B*

3 VOCABULARY drinks

Write the names of the drinks.

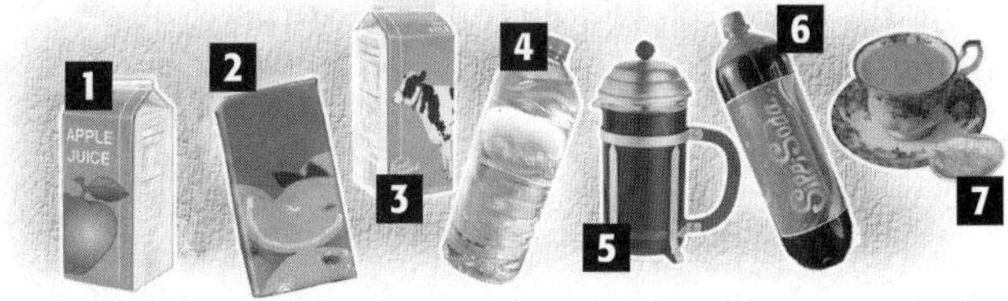

1 *apple juice* 4 __________ 6 __________
2 __________ 5 __________ 7 __________
3 __________

4 VOCABULARY "water" reading

Complete the sentences with these words.

temperature at least ~~sweat~~ contain
experiments in fact myth

1 When you're hot, you *sweat* to reduce your body heat.
2 We don't always need to drink a lot of water. __________ sometimes one liter a day is OK.
3 The __________ in Madrid in August is very high.
4 Scientists are doing __________ to find a cure for the common cold.
5 Candy and chocolate __________ a lot of calories.
6 Some people say you need to drink __________ two liters of water a day.
7 It's a __________ that coffee and soda make you thirsty – it's just not true!

More Words to Learn

Write translations and try to remember the words.

Word	Pronunciation	Translation
liters *noun*	/ˈlitərs/	
tap *noun*	/tæp/	
lose *verb*	/luz/	
agree *verb*	/əˈgri/	
probably *adverb*	/ˈprɑbəbli/	
like *preposition*	/laɪk/	
a bottle of...	/eɪ ˈbɑtl əv/	
of course	/əv kɔrs/	
more or less	/mɔr ər lɛs/	
for example	/fər ɪgˈzæmpl/	

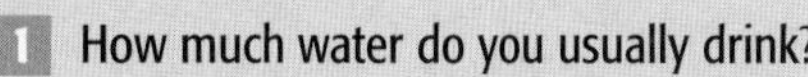

Can you answer these questions?

1 How much water do you usually drink?
2 How many cookies do you eat a week?
3 How much television do you watch?
4 How much money do you spend on clothes?
5 How many very good friends do you have?

Study Link **MultiROM**

To travel hopefully is a better thing than to arrive.
Robert Louis Stevenson, Scottish writer

Trading vacations

1 GRAMMAR *be going to* (plans)

a Order the words to make sentences.

1 going / She / vacation / enjoy / 's / the / to
She's going to enjoy the vacation.

2 to / aren't / We / a / going / stay / in / hotel
________________________________.

3 going / They / to / go / 're / swimming
________________________________.

4 'm / I / go / camping / going / to
________________________________.

5 you / to / Are / trip / for / going / pay / the
________________________________?

6 isn't / see / the / He / to / going / pyramids
________________________________.

b Complete the sentences. Use *going to*.

1 What time *are they going to leave* (they / leave) tomorrow?

2 We ________________ (try) the local food.

3 They ________________ (have) dinner with their friends this weekend.

4 ________________ (you / stay) at an expensive hotel?

5 They ________________ (not / get married) until next year.

6 ________________ (they / see) the Statue of Liberty?

7 He ________________ (meet) a lot of people.

8 She ________________ (not / go) on vacation this year.

c Complete the dialogue. Use *going to*.

A So, where 1 *are you going to go* (go) on vacation?

B We 2 ________________ (travel) around Europe by train.

A That sounds great. Which countries 3 ________________ (visit)?

B Italy first, and then Croatia, Greece, and Turkey.

A Where 4 ________________ (sleep)?

B Well, we 5 ________________ (not / stay) in hotels! We don't have much money. We can sleep on the train. The only problem is that it 6 ________________ (be) very hot.

A And where 7 ________________ (go) after Italy?

B After Italy we 8 ________________ (get) the train to Zagreb. Then Makiko 9 ________________ (come) home, and I 10 ________________ (go) to Greece. I want to visit Athens. Then I 11 ________________ (spend) a week on a Greek island before I go to Turkey. I 12 ________________ (not / get) home until the end of August.

Study Link **Student Book p.134** *Grammar Bank 7C*

2 PRONUNCIATION word stress

a Underline the stressed syllable in these words. How many are not stressed on the first syllable?

1 couple	4 weather	7 nightlife
2 hotel	5 museum	8 vacation
3 campsite	6 restaurant	

b Practice saying the words.

3 **VOCABULARY** vacations

Write the expressions in the correct column.

on vacation · the sights · ~~in a hotel~~ · shopping · to the beach · at a campsite · in a bed and breakfast · a show · the Statue of Liberty

STAY	GO	SEE
in a hotel		

4 **READING**

a Read the advertisements.

★Four *dream* vacations★
★ for the 21st century ★

A See a penguin

This is a once-in-a-lifetime vacation in the snow and ice of the Antarctic. You visit the isolated places the great explorers discovered, and you can see animals and birds you only normally see on TV or in zoos. The trip starts in South Africa and finishes in Western Australia. You travel on a Russian ship, *Kapitan Khlebnikov*, and the vacation lasts for just under a month.

B Go on a safari

This vacation is a safari with a difference. You travel by helicopter over parts of Kenya, listening to classical music as you fly. Then you sleep under the African stars in a luxury bed. There's another trip, this time in a hot-air balloon for two people, which gives you a second chance to see wild animals in their natural habitat. The best moment is the Elephant Watch in Samburu, where your experienced guide can tell you all about these amazing animals.

C Fly high

This is probably the most expensive vacation in the world. You can go on a flight into space and orbit the Earth in a spaceship – if you have the money! The only problem with this vacation is the six-day training course before you take the trip. You travel 60 miles above the Earth for between 30 and 90 minutes, and you get a beautiful view of our green and blue planet.

D Live like Robinson Crusoe

If you dream of life on a desert island, this is the vacation for you. The island of Quilalea is off the coast of Mozambique, and the only inhabitants are turtles and a few tourists. You can live like Robinson Crusoe: watch the turtles, go fishing, or sail to another island to have a picnic.

Adapted from a newspaper

b Read the text again and match the tourists to a vacation.

1 A millionaire looking for something to tell his friends.
2 A rich couple who like animals and hot weather.
3 A strong, young scientist who enjoys cold weather.
4 A group of friends who want to forget about their stressful jobs.

c Read the text again and label the pictures.

1 *penguin* 2 ______ 3 ______

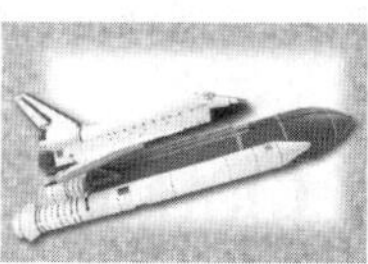

4 ______ 5 ______ 6 ______

More Words to Learn

Write translations and try to remember the words.

Word	Pronunciation	Translation
couple *noun*	/ˈkʌpl/	
minute *noun*	/ˈmɪnət/	
(see the) sights *noun*	/saɪts/	
campsite *noun*	/ˈkæmpsaɪt/	
nightlife *noun*	/ˈnaɪtlaɪf/	
disaster *noun*	/dɪˈzæstər/	
boat *noun*	/boʊt/	
ideal *adjective*	/aɪˈdiəl/	
plan *verb*	/plæn/	
go camping *verb*	/ˈkæmpɪŋ/	

QUESTION TIME

Can you answer these questions?

1 Where are you going to go on vacation this year?
2 What are you going to see there?
3 What are you going to do there?
4 Who are you going to go with?
5 How much is it going to cost you?

Study Link MultiROM

Love cannot save you from your own fate.
Jim Morrison, singer of The Doors

It's written in the cards

1 VOCABULARY verb phrases

Complete with verbs from the box. Sometimes more than one answer is possible.

be have get fall move meet

1 *be* famous
2 ______ a surprise
3 ______ married
4 ______ lucky
5 ______ in love
6 ______ to another country
7 ______ a lot of money
8 ______ out of a house
9 ______ a new job
10 ______ somebody new
11 ______ a baby

2 GRAMMAR *be going to* (predictions)

a Look at the picture and write sentences using these verbs and *be going to*.

buy ~~eat~~ take fall get drink make see

1 *She's going to eat* her ice cream.
2 ______ off his bike.
3 ______ a taxi.
4 ______ some water.
5 ______ a movie.
6 ______ a photo.
7 ______ a newspaper.
8 ______ a sandwich.

b Write a letter in the box: A = plan, B = prediction.

1 I'm going to buy some souvenirs in the gift shop. [A]
2 You're going to be hot in that jacket. [ ]
3 My cousin is going to get married in the spring. [ ]
4 We're going to be late if we don't hurry. [ ]
5 There's going to be a beautiful sunset tonight. [ ]
6 I think that factory's going to close. [ ]
7 They're going to buy a new car. [ ]
8 I'm going to book a flight tomorrow. [ ]

Study Link **Student Book p.134** *Grammar Bank 7D*

3 PRONUNCIATION /ʊ/, /u/, and /ʌ/

a Match the words to sounds 1, 2, and 3. Then connect the words that have the same sound.

1  2 u 3 ʌ

1 **goo**d	st**u**dent
l**o**ve	m**o**ney
m**u**sic	c**oo**k

h**u**ngry	b**oo**k
n**ew**spaper	l**u**nch
l**oo**king	tr**ue**

b Practice saying the words.

c Complete the dialogues by using the pairs of matching words from exercise **a**.

1 Does your husband make the dinner?
Yes, he's a very *good* *cook*.

2 What are the most important things in life?
__________ and __________.

3 What do you do?
I'm a __________ __________.

4 Can I help you?
Yes, I'm __________ for a __________ about Italy.

5 A lot of the things you read in the __________ are often not __________.

6 I'm __________. What's for __________?

d Practice reading the dialogues.

More Words to Learn

Write translations and try to remember the words.

Word	Pronunciation	Translation
surprise *noun*	/sərˈpraɪz/	
heart *noun*	/hɑrt/	
ring *noun*	/rɪŋ/	
voice *noun*	/vɔɪs/	
card *noun*	/kɑrd/	
(I'm) sure *adjective*	/ʃʊr/	
put *verb*	/pʊt/	
maybe *adverb*	/ˈmeɪbi/	
soon *adverb*	/sun/	

QUESTION TIME

Can you answer these questions?

1 What are you going to do this weekend?
2 Are you going to travel this year?
3 Are you going to get married this year?
4 What are you going to have for dinner this evening?
5 Are you going to start a new job this year?

Study Link MultiROM

CAN YOU REMEMBER...? FILES 6&7

Complete each sentence with one word.

1 There __________ any cupboards in the kitchen, but there are some shelves.
2 __________ there many people at the soccer game last night?
3 Oh no! The baby __________ crying again.
4 She usually __________ pants, but today she's wearing a skirt.
5 There's __________ milk in the fridge if you want it.
6 How __________ sandwiches do you want?
7 We're __________ to visit our cousins this weekend.
8 When __________ you going to get married?

7 At a restaurant

1 VOCABULARY AND READING

a Look at the menu and answer the questions.

1 Which is the best appetizer for somebody on a diet?
2 What main course can a vegetarian have?
3 Can you have fruit for dessert?
4 How many types of drinks are there?
5 Do children pay the same as adults?

Seaview Restaurant Menu

Appetizers

Soup of the day $4.50 — Grilled low-fat goat cheese (V) $5.00
Smoked salmon $7.95

Salads

Mixed salad (V) $6.50 — Seafood salad $11.25

Main courses

Fillet steak, served with French fries and carrots $14.75
Summer vegetable omelette (V) $8.50
Grilled tuna, served with a choice of fresh vegetables $13.25

Desserts

Cheesecake $4.95 — Selection of ice cream $3.50
Cheese and fruit $7.95

Beverages

Glass of wine (red or white) $6.50 — Beer $5.25
Bottle of wine (red or white) $32.00 — Soft drinks $2.00
Coffee $1.50

Set menu

$12.50 (see the board for today's choice)

25% discount on children's portions — Service charge is included
(V) vegetarian

b Match the words and the definitions.

1 service charge [*f*]
2 set menu [ ]
3 bookings [ ]
4 discount [ ]
5 beverages [ ]
6 soft drinks [ ]

a drinks
b reservations
c reduced price
d soda
e a limited menu – you pay a fixed price and everything is included
f ~~extra money you pay for the waiters~~

c Underline five words or phrases you don't know. Use your dictionary to look up their meaning and pronunciation.

2 ORDERING A MEAL

Complete the dialogue with one word in each blank.

A Good evening. Do you have a 1 *reservation* ?
B Yes, a 2 ________ for two. My name's John McGeever.
A 3 ________ or non-smoking?
B Non-smoking, please.
A Come this way, please.

A Are you ready to 4 ________ ?
B Yes, 5 ________ like the mushroom risotto.
C Chicken salad 6 ________ me, please.
A What would you 7 ________ to drink?
B An orange 8 ________ , please.

3 SOCIAL ENGLISH

Complete the dialogue with phrases a–e.

a Could we have the check, please?
b ~~It was delicious.~~
c The same for me, please.
d Nothing for me, thanks.
e What is there?

A Was the pasta good?
B Yes, thanks. 1 *b*
WAITER Would you like dessert?
B Yes, please. 2 ________
WAITER Ice cream with chocolate sauce or fruit salad.
B The ice cream for me, please.
WAITER And you, sir?
A 3 ________
WAITER Here you are. Would you like any coffee?
B Yes, a cappuccino please.
A 4 ________
WAITER Two cappuccinos. Anything else?
A No, thank you. 5 ________

The True False Show

Imagination is more important than knowledge.
Albert Einstein, German scientist

1 GRAMMAR comparative adjectives

a Write the comparative forms of these adjectives in the correct circle.

~~beautiful~~ dirty cold high wet cheap good dry hungry thin sad difficult bad comfortable far

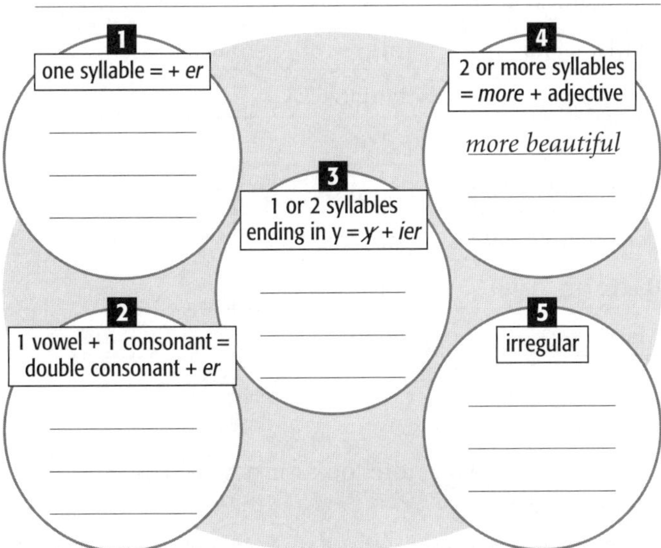

b Write sentences using the opposite adjective.

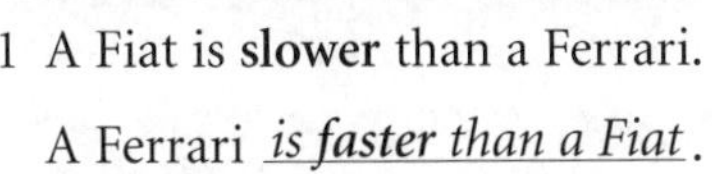

1 A Fiat is **slower** than a Ferrari.
A Ferrari *is faster than a Fiat*.

2 The Pacific Ocean is **bigger** than the Atlantic Ocean.
The Atlantic Ocean ______________________.

3 Germany is **wetter** than Tunisia.
Tunisia ______________________.

4 The Suez Canal is **longer** than the Panama Canal.
The Panama Canal ______________________.

5 Gold is **more expensive** than silver.
Silver ______________________.

6 Olive oil is **better** for you than butter.
Butter ______________________.

7 The sun is **hotter** than the moon.
The moon ______________________.

8 English is **easier** than Chinese.
Chinese ______________________.

Study Link **Student Book p.136** *Grammar Bank 8A*

2 PRONUNCIATION vowel sounds

a Write the words in the chart.

wo**r**se slo**w**er dr**i**er ~~easier~~ h**ea**lthier d**ir**tier m**o**re b**e**tter c**o**lder che**a**per h**igh**er sh**or**ter

ɪ	ɜr	ər	ɛ	oʊ	aɪ
easier	____	____	____	____	____
____	____	____	____	____	____

b Practice saying the words.

3 VOCABULARY personality adjectives

Complete the sentences with these words.

aggressive stylish generous quiet careful ~~serious~~ friendly

1 Mark reads lots of books about politics. He's *serious*.
2 Maria likes buying people presents. She's __________.
3 Caroline wears really nice clothes. She's __________.
4 Jeanine loves going to parties and talking to people.
She's __________.
5 Paulo argues a lot. He's __________.
6 Lana plans things for a long time before she does them.
She's __________.
7 Ted never says very much. He's __________.

4 READING

a What do you think are the perfect colors to paint your apartment or house? Look at the chart and complete column 1 with a color from the box.

blue   red/orange   green/white   yellow

Rooms	1 My opinion	2 The expert's opinion
Bedroom		
Living room		
Dining room		
Office		

b Now read the text and complete column 2 (The expert's opinion). Do you agree?

Perfect colors, Perfect harmony

The color you paint the rooms in your house can make you more comfortable. Follow the suggestions below to create the perfect atmosphere to eat, sleep, work, and relax in your own home.

The bedroom
The perfect color for a bedroom is blue. It is a very relaxing color, and can make you feel happier and more positive about life when you wake up in the morning.

The living room
The perfect color for an elegant living room is green, with some white. Don't use dramatic colors like red, purple, and black because they don't help you relax.

The dining room
Red and orange are two colors that can make you feel hungrier at mealtimes. They also encourage more interesting conversation. But be careful! Only use these colors in small areas – a lot of red or orange can make you feel aggressive.

The office
Yellow is a beautiful color that makes you feel happier and helps you to think, so it is a good color for this room. It also makes dark spaces a little brighter.

c Look at the highlighted words. What do you think they mean? Check the ones you don't know in your dictionary.

d Read the text again. Mark the sentences T (true) or F (false).

1 A blue bedroom helps you wake up earlier. *F*
2 Green and white are dramatic colors. ___
3 Red or orange in the dining room makes people eat and talk. ___
4 A yellow office helps you work better. ___

More Words to Learn

Write translations and try to remember the words.

Word	Pronunciation	Translation
mosquitoes *noun*	/mə'skitoʊz/	
sharks *noun*	/ʃɑrks/	
tigers *noun*	/'taɪgərz/	
adult *noun*	/ə'dʌlt/	
(make) jokes *noun*	/dʒoʊks/	
personality *noun*	/pərsə'næləti/	
the Earth *noun*	/ərθ/	
Mars *noun*	/mɑrz/	

Study idea

Start a vocabulary notebook for new words you want to learn.

1 Write a translation, and use your dictionary to check the pronunciation.
2 Underline the stressed syllable.

Word	Translation
contestant	concursante

QUESTION TIME

Can you answer these questions?

1 Is your country bigger than the US?
2 Is it hotter or colder than the US?
3 Is it wetter or drier than the US?
4 Is it safer or more dangerous than the US?
5 Is it cheaper or more expensive than the US?

Study Link MultiROM

The coldest winter I ever spent was a summer in San Francisco.
Mark Twain, American writer

The highest city in the world

1 GRAMMAR superlative adjectives

a Complete the chart.

adjective	comparative	superlative
cold	*colder*	*the coldest*
high		
expensive		
dry		
dangerous		
hot		
beautiful		
crowded		
good		
bad		

b Write the questions.

1 What / long river / world?
What's the longest river in the world?
2 What / small country / world?
______
3 What / crowded country / world?
______
4 What / high mountain / world?
______
5 What / windy city / world?
______
6 What / small ocean / world?
______
7 What / expensive mineral / world?
______
8 What / dry place / world?
______

c Circle the correct answer to the questions in exercise **b**.

1 a (The Nile)
b The Danube
c The Amazon

2 a Andorra
b Monaco
c The Vatican

3 a India
b Bangladesh
c China

4 a Mount Everest
b Mont Blanc
c Mount Kilimanjaro

5 a Chicago, US
b La Paz, Bolivia
c Edinburgh, Scotland

6 a The Arctic Ocean
b The Atlantic Ocean
c The Pacific Ocean

7 a platinum
b diamond
c graphite

8 a The Sahara Desert
b The Atacama Desert, Chile
c The Arizona Desert, US

d Write superlative sentences. Use the information in the chart.

Hotel	Size	Popular	Beautiful	Price
Minerva, Rome	24 rooms	☺☺☺	☺☺☺☺	$250 per night
Seine Palace, Paris	36 rooms	☺☺	☺☺☺	$210 per night
Victoria Inn, London	18 rooms	☺	☺☺	$225 per night
Rio Club, Rio de Janeiro	60 rooms	☺☺☺☺	☺☺☺	$180 per night

1 big *The Rio Club is the biggest.*
2 small ______.
3 popular ______.
4 cheap ______.
5 expensive ______.
6 beautiful ______.

Study Link **Student Book p.136** *Grammar Bank 8B*

2 VOCABULARY the weather

Complete the sentences with a word from the box.

sunny	wet	~~hot~~	snowing	dry	cold
cloudy	windy				

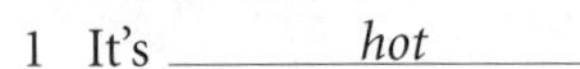

1 It's ___hot___.

2 It's ________.

3 It's ________.

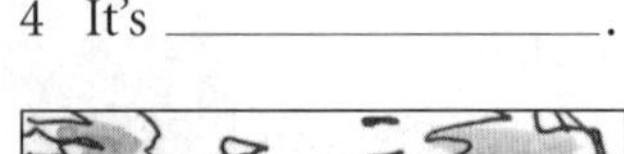

4 It's ________.

5 It's ________.

6 It's ________.

7 It's ________.

8 It's ________.

3 PRONUNCIATION consonant groups

a Underline the stressed syllables.

1 the most difficult
2 the noisiest
3 the most expensive
4 the fastest
5 the coldest
6 the most crowded
7 the most beautiful
8 the driest

b Practice saying the phrases.

More Words to Learn

Write translations and try to remember the words.

Word	Pronunciation	Translation
oxygen *noun*	/ˈɑksɪdʒən/	
altitude *noun*	/ˈæltətud/	
air conditioning *noun*	/ɛr kənˈdɪʃnɪŋ/	
capital *noun*	/ˈkæpətl/	
geography *noun*	/dʒiˈɑgrəfi/	
climate *noun*	/ˈklaɪmet/	
crowded *adjective*	/ˈkraʊdəd/	
boring *adjective*	/ˈbɔrɪŋ/	
imagine *verb*	/ɪˈmædʒən/	
surprisingly *adverb*	/sərˈpraɪzɪŋli/	

QUESTION TIME

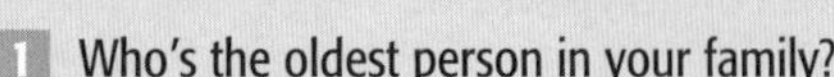

Can you answer these questions?

1 Who's the oldest person in your family?
2 Who's the tallest person in your family?
3 Who's the most intelligent person in your family?
4 Who's the best-looking person in your family?
5 Who's the worst driver in your family?

Study Link **MultiROM**

Study Link www.oup.com/elt/americanenglishfile/1

I'd like to live like a poor man, but with a lot of money.
Pablo Picasso, Spanish painter

8C Would you like to drive a Ferrari?

1 GRAMMAR *would like to / like*

a Write the contractions.

1 He would like to see the movie again.
He'd like to see the movie again.

2 She would like to do a parachute jump.
________________________________.

3 They would not like to go skiing.
________________________________.

4 I would like to learn Chinese.
________________________________.

5 We would not like to work in a fast-food restaurant.
________________________________.

6 He would like to be lucky one day.
________________________________.

7 You would not like to see that movie.
________________________________.

b Write sentences or questions with *would like.* Use contractions.

1 he / be a teacher (–)
He wouldn't like to be a teacher.

2 you / be a ballet dancer (?)
________________________________?

3 we / live in a big city (+)
________________________________.

4 I / learn how to fly a plane (+)
________________________________.

5 she / work for that company (–)
________________________________.

6 they / go to Chile on vacation (?)
________________________________?

c Choose the correct question.

1 **A** Do you like going for a walk? ✗
Would you like to go for a walk? ✓
B No, not now. I'm tired.

2 **A** Would you like a cookie?
Do you like a cookie?
B Yes, please. I'm very hungry.

3 **A** Do you like your neighbors?
Would you like your neighbors?
B Yes, they're very friendly.

4 **A** What do you like doing tonight?
What would you like to do tonight?
B Let's go to the movies.

5 **A** Would you like to go to the beach?
Do you like going to the beach?
B No, I don't. I don't like the sun.

d Circle the correct answer.

1 I'd like (**to learn**) / **learning** to dance salsa.
2 What does David like **do** / **doing** in his free time?
3 Do you like **cook** / **cooking**?
4 Would you like **to come** / **coming** to dinner tonight?
5 I wouldn't like **to go up** / **going up** in a hot-air balloon.
6 I don't like **fly** / **flying**.

Study Link **Student Book p.136** *Grammar Bank 8C*

2 PRONUNCIATION sentence stress

a Underline the stressed words.

1 A Would you like to drive a sports car?
B Yes, I'd love to.
A Why?
B Because I love cars, and I love driving.

2 A Would you like to ride a horse?
B No, I wouldn't.
A Why not?
B Because I don't like horses.

b Practice saying the dialogues.

3 READING

a Read the text and write a letter in each space.

Which adventure experience...

1 ... can your family also enjoy? *B*
2 ... teaches you how to make your house more comfortable? ___
3 ... helps you when you go to a restaurant? ___
4 ... gives you a free meal? ___
5 ... is not for people who don't like alcohol? ___
6 ... is not for people who can't swim? ___

b Look at the highlighted words. What do you think they mean? Check with your dictionary.

Presents to remember

A Wine tasting

This is the perfect experience for stylish people who want to know the difference between a good wine and a bad wine. You can learn a lot about wine and how it is made with the help of the experts, and you can try some excellent wines. After this course you will know which wine to buy in the supermarket and which wine to order in a restaurant.

B Waterskiing

If you're a good swimmer, why not try waterskiing? First, you do a quick training course on land. Then you're ready to practice in the water. This activity is really exciting, and your friends and family can have a good time watching, too.

C Interior design tuition

If you want to change the style of your house, but you don't know where to start, this is the present for you. Professional designers teach you how to use space, light, and color. They also help you be more creative by introducing your own personal style into your designs. Lunch is included in the course.

More Words to Learn

Write translations and try to remember the words.

Word	Pronunciation	Translation
dreams *noun*	/drimz/	
weight *noun*	/weɪt/	
height *noun*	/haɪt/	
experience *noun*	/ɪk'spɪriəns/	
adventure *noun*	/əd'vɛntʃər/	
chef *noun*	/ʃɛf/	
jump *verb*	/dʒʌmp/	
last *verb*	/læst/	
suddenly *adverb*	/'sʌdnli/	
including *preposition*	/ɪn'kludɪŋ/	

QUESTION TIME

Can you answer these questions?

1 Do you like doing dangerous sports?
2 Would you like to do a parachute jump?
3 What would you like for your birthday?
4 Where would you like to go on vacation this year?
5 Which countries would you like to visit?

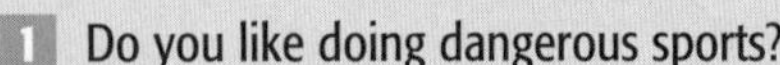

Study Link MultiROM

It is totally impossible to be well dressed in cheap shoes.
Hardy Amies, British fashion designer

They dress well but drive badly

1 GRAMMAR adverbs

a Complete the sentences with an adverb.

1 The Germans are careful drivers.
They drive *carefully* .
2 The French cook perfect meals.
They cook ________.
3 The British are very polite.
They speak very ________.
4 The Brazilians are good at soccer.
They play soccer ________.
5 The Japanese are very hard workers.
They work very ________.
6 The Swedish speak beautiful English.
They speak English ________.

b Make adverbs from the adjectives and complete the sentences.

good careful hard
loud stylish ~~happy~~
generous beautiful

The ideal partner...
1 ...does housework *happily* .
2 ...dances ________.
3 ...cooks ________.
4 ...dresses ________.
5 ...drives ________.
6 ...gives presents ________.
7 ...works ________.
8 ...never speaks ________.

c Circle the correct answer.
1 My brother's a very **careful** / **carefully** driver.
2 Frank cooks very **good** / **well**.
3 Elena wears very **stylish** / **stylishly** clothes.
4 He always speaks very **aggressive** / **aggressively** to me.
5 He's very **quiet** / **quietly**. He never says anything!
6 She's **generous** / **generously**. She gives nice presents.
7 My Korean is very **bad** / **badly**.
8 Can you speak more **slow** / **slowly**?

Study Link **Student Book p.136** *Grammar Bank 8D*

2 PRONUNCIATION adjectives and adverbs

a Underline the stressed syllables.

1 badly
2 dangerously
3 beautifully
4 politely
5 carefully
6 slowly
7 completely
8 quietly
9 stylishly

b Practice saying the words.

3 READING

a Read the story, and put the pictures in the correct order.

Romance…without a ring!

A couple from Colorado, in the US, had a big surprise last Saturday when they lost a $4,000 ring at the top of a mountain.

Derek Monnig, 33, bought the diamond ring for his girlfriend, Debra Sweeney, 34, to celebrate their engagement. He wanted to ask her to marry him in a very romantic place, so they walked slowly in the snow to the top of the Rocky Mountains. They stopped and Derek said, "I have something for you. Honey, I love you. Will you marry me?"

Suddenly, he took the ring out of his pocket and started to put it on her finger. But the ring fell into the snow near Debra's boots. They started to look for it, and other people came quickly to help them, but they couldn't find it, so they called the ski patrol. Seven more people came to help. They spent two hours with them trying to find the ring. The next day, the couple went back to the mountain with a metal detector, but they never found it.

Debra wasn't too unhappy. "It's much better to lose the ring than the guy," she said. And luckily the ring was insured.

Adapted from a website

b Write T (true) or F (false).

1 Derek and Debra wanted to get married on top of a mountain. *F*
2 Derek had the ring in his pocket. __
3 The ring fell into one of Debra's boots. __
4 Seven people in all helped them look for the ring. __
5 They spent all day looking for the ring. __
6 The couple went back again with a metal detector. __

c Guess the meaning of the highlighted words. Then check your dictionary.

More Words to Learn

Write translations and try to remember the words.

Word	Pronunciation	Translation
social life *noun*	/ˈsoʊʃl laɪf/	
crime *noun*	/kraɪm/	
shy *adjective*	/ʃaɪ/	
polite *adjective*	/pəˈlaɪt/	
elegant *adjective*	/ˈɛləgənt/	
steal *verb*	/stil/	
dress *verb*	/drɛs/	
everywhere *adverb*	/ˈɛvriwɛr/	
abroad *adverb*	/əˈbrɔd/	
almost *adverb*	/ˈɔlmoʊst/	

QUESTION TIME

Can you answer these questions?

1 Do you speak English well or badly?
2 Do you dress stylishly?
3 Do you drive fast or slowly?
4 Do you speak quietly or loudly?
5 Do you play any sports very well?

Study Link MultiROM

CAN YOU REMEMBER…? FILES 7&8

Complete each sentence with one word.

1 Is there ________ sugar in this coffee?
2 How ________ money do you have with you?
3 Who are you ________ to go on vacation with?
4 I think ________ is going to rain.
5 His office is bigger ________ mine.
6 Who's ________ tallest person in your family?
7 I ________ like to do a parachute jump. I don't like flying.
8 My father drives very ________. He never goes more than 30 mph.

8 Going home

1 VOCABULARY verb phrases

Match the phrases.

1 I'd like to [*b*] a a taxi?
2 Could I have [ ] b ~~check out.~~
3 Can I pay [ ] c help with your luggage?
4 Please sign [ ] d by credit card?
5 Do you need any [ ] e your name here.
6 Can you call me [ ] f the bill, please?

2 CHECKING OUT

Order the dialogue.

B Of course. [ ]
B Room 223. [ ]
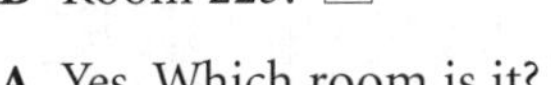
A Yes. Which room is it? [ ]
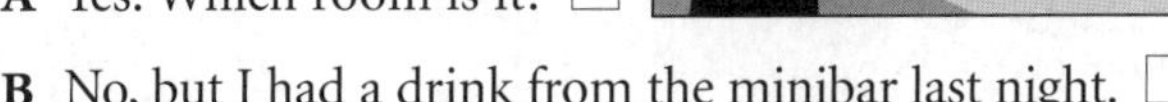
B No, but I had a drink from the minibar last night. [ ]
A Thank you very much. Have a good trip. [ ]
A Good morning, ma'am. [*1*]
B Morning. Can I have the bill, please? [*2*]
A OK, can you sign here, please? [ ]
A Did you make any phone calls? [ ]
B Thank you. Good-bye. [ ]

3 SOCIAL ENGLISH

Complete the sentences with a phrase from the box.

a good trip	can we meet	~~I'll call~~
I'll meet you	I'll e-mail you	I'm late

A Oh no, I'm going to be late for my train.
B Don't worry. 1 *I'll call* a taxi.

A 2 ______________ at the airport.
B OK. Where 3 ______________?
A At the information desk at 7 o'clock.

A Sorry 4 ______________.
B No problem. We have time.

A Have 5 ______________. And please write.
B 6 ______________ next week, I promise.

4 READING

a Read the text about Chicago O'Hare.

CHICAGO O'HARE INTERNATIONAL AIRPORT

Chicago O'Hare International Airport is one of the busiest airports in the world, and 75 million passengers pass through it every year. Below you can find four different ways of getting to the airport:

BY CAR
O'Hare Airport is 18 miles (29 km) northwest of downtown Chicago. If you are planning to drive to the airport from downtown Chicago, you need to take Interstate I-90 west to Interstate I-190, and then follow the signs to O'Hare Airport. It takes approximately 30–45 minutes to drive to O'Hare from downtown Chicago.

BY TRAIN
The Chicago Transit Authority offers 24-hour train service on the Blue Line to O'Hare Airport from downtown Chicago. The trains run every ten minutes, 24 hours a day. The trip from downtown Chicago takes about 45 minutes.

BY BUS/VAN
Continental Airport Express offers pick-up service from most downtown Chicago hotels. The vans will drop you off in front of your terminal. The fare is $18, and the trip takes about 45 minutes.

BY TAXI
Call Checker Cab for a taxi to take you to O'Hare. The cost of a taxi ride from downtown is about $40. The trip takes approximately 30–45 minutes, depending on traffic.

b How did the following people get to the airport?

1 James went on the highway. *by car*
2 Sarah paid $40. ______
3 Robert took the Blue Line. ______
4 Leo was picked up at his hotel. ______

c Underline five words or phrases you don't know. Use your dictionary to look up their meaning and pronunciation.

O, beware, my lord, of jealousy! It is the green-eyed monster…

William Shakespeare, English dramatist

9A Before we met

1 VOCABULARY "jealous" reading

Complete the sentences with these words.

vacation brochure ~~reply~~ silence fun pick up

1 I asked him a question, but he didn't *reply*.

2 **A** How did you find this hotel?

B I saw it in a __________.

3 I like walking in the mountains – I love the __________.

4 Could you __________ those papers, please?

5 **A** Did you have a good time at the party last night?

B Yes, it was __________.

2 GRAMMAR present perfect

a Write the contractions.

1 I have not been to Thailand.

I haven't been to Thailand.

2 Tim has not been to a Japanese restaurant.

____

3 We have been to this city before.

____

4 I have been to this club lots of times.

____

5 They have not been to New York.

____

6 My girlfriend has been to Paris twice.

____

7 He has been to Peru.

____

8 We have not been to Mexico.

____

b Write sentences.

1 Brazil *She's been to Brazil.*

2 Australia *They've been to Australia.*

3 Japan ____________________.

4 Thailand ____________________.

5 Canada ____________________.

6 China ____________________.

7 Malaysia ____________________.

8 Argentina ____________________.

c Complete the dialogue.

A Have you [1] *been* to the US?

B No, I [2] __________, but my wife has.

A Where [3] __________ she been in the US?

B Only New York.

A Has she [4] __________ to Canada?

B No, she [5] __________. But we'd like to go there one day.

A And [6] __________ you been to Australia?

B No, I [7] __________. Have you?

A Yes, I [8] __________. I've been to Sydney and Canberra.

Study Link **Student Book p.138** *Grammar Bank 9A*

3 VOCABULARY town and city

Where have these people been? Complete the sentences.

1 She's been to the m*arket*_____.

2 He's been to the b__________.

3 They've been to the t__________.

4 He's been to the s__________.

5 She's been to the h__________.

6 He's been to the s________ c________.

7 She's been to the p__________.

8 They've been to the t________ a________.

Study Link Student Book p.152 *Vocabulary Bank*

4 PRONUNCIATION

Circle the word with a different sound. Practice saying the words.

ɑ	**o**pera	st**o**p	c**o**ncert	(c**ou**ntry)
ər	Th**ur**sday	m**ar**ket	g**ir**lfriend	p**er**son
ɛ	j**ea**lous	n**e**ver	br**ea**k	t**e**ll
k	**c**ity	**c**ontinent	**k**arao**k**e	pi**ck** up
dʒ	**J**une	**G**ermany	travel a**g**ent	an**g**ry
h	**h**ave	**h**oliday	**h**our	**h**otel

More Words to Learn

Write translations and try to remember the words.

Word	Pronunciation	Translation
sports event *noun*	/spɔrts ɪˈvɛnt/	
continent *noun*	/ˈkɑntənənt/	
spa *noun*	/spɑ/	
miles *noun*	/maɪlz/	
silence *noun*	/ˈsaɪləns/	
jealous *adjective*	/ˈdʒɛləs/	
exactly *adverb*	/ɪgˈzæktli/	
somewhere *adverb*	/ˈsʌmwɛr/	

Study idea

Look back at the eight **Study ideas** in this workbook. Which ones do you do?

QUESTION TIME

Can you answer these questions?

1 Have you been to work today?
2 Have you been to the supermarket today?
3 Have you been to a restaurant today?
4 Have you been to the movies today?
5 Have you been to a friend's house today?

Study Link MultiROM

Movies should have a beginning, a middle, and an end – but not necessarily in that order.
Jean-Luc Godard, French movie director

9B I've read the book, I've seen the movie

1 VOCABULARY past participles

a Write the past participles of these irregular verbs.

base form	simple past	past participle
break	broke	*broken*
buy	bought	
drive	drove	
find	found	
give	gave	
lose	lost	
make	made	
run	ran	
write	wrote	

b Use past participles from the chart to complete the sentences.

1 Debbie and Fernando have *bought* a new house.
2 I've never __________ a marathon.
3 Daniel has __________ his girlfriend some flowers.
4 John Grisham has __________ many bestsellers.
5 Have you ever __________ your leg?
6 I'm going to be late. I've __________ the car keys.
7 You've __________ a lot of mistakes.
8 She's __________ some money in the street.
9 I've never __________ a Ferrari.

2 PRONUNCIATION irregular participles

Circle the word with a different vowel sound. Practice saying the words.

ɪ	ɔ	ɛ	ʌ	eɪ	oʊ
given	found	left	come	taken	known
written	thought	gave	done	made	lost
(seen)	caught	said	drunk	read	broken
driven	drawn	sent	got	paid	spoken

3 GRAMMAR present perfect or simple past?

a Circle the correct form.

1 I (**didn't meet**) / **have never met** anyone nice at the party.
2 Miko **went / has been** to the movies last weekend.
3 **Did you read / Have you read** any books by John Irving?
4 Lucy's a journalist. She **met / has met** a lot of interesting people.
5 They **started / have started** to watch the movie, but they fell asleep before the end.
6 We **didn't see / haven't seen** the movie yesterday because the theater was full.
7 I **didn't read / haven't read** any Terry Pratchett books. I don't like science fiction.
8 **Did you go / Have you been** to that new restaurant downtown last Saturday?

b Complete the dialogues with the correct form of the verbs in parentheses.

A 1 *Have you read* (read) any of the Harry Potter books?
B Yes, I have. My brother 2__________ (give) them to me for my last birthday.
A Which one 3__________ you __________ (like) best?
B The first one. I 4__________ (read) it five times.

A 5__________ you __________ (see) the new Almodóvar movie?
B Yes, I have. I 6__________ (take) my boyfriend to see it last night.
A 7__________ (be) it good?
B No, I 8__________ __________ (not / enjoy) it.

Study Link Student Book p.138 *Grammar Bank 9B*

The richest woman in the UK is now Joanne Kathleen Rowling, the author of the Harry Potter books. But life hasn't always been easy for her.

She was born on July 31st, 1965 and started writing at the early age of six. At school, she was very quiet and didn't like sports much. Her favorite subjects were English and Modern Languages. After school, she studied French at Exeter University, and she later became a bilingual secretary. She didn't enjoy her life as a secretary, and when she was 26 she left the UK to teach English in Portugal. She met and married a journalist and their daughter, Jessica, was born in 1993. The marriage ended in divorce and Ms. Rowling moved to Edinburgh, Scotland. It was during this period that she started her first Harry Potter novel, which she wrote in a cafe while her daughter was asleep.

She published *Harry Potter and the Philosopher's Stone* in 1997, and in the same year she won one of the most important book awards in Britain. Since then millions of people have read her books in many different languages, and millions have seen the Harry Potter movies. Everybody knows who she is and everybody has heard of the famous character she has created. Harry Potter is possibly the most famous boy in the world.

Adapted from a website

Read the text and answer the questions.

1 When was J. K. Rowling born?
2 How old was she when she started writing?
3 What were her favorite subjects at school?
4 What two jobs did she do before she became a writer?
5 Why did she go to Portugal?
6 What does her ex-husband do?
7 When was her daughter born?
8 Where did she write the first Harry Potter novel?
9 When did she win a book award?
10 How many people have read her books and seen the movies?

More Words to Learn

Write translations and try to remember the words.

Word	Pronunciation	Translation
back row *noun*	/bæk roʊ/	
soundtrack *noun*	/ˈsaʊndtræk/	
autograph *noun*	/ˈɔtəgræf/	
bestseller *noun*	/bɛstˈsɛlər/	
version *noun*	/ˈvərʒn/	
prefer *verb*	/prɪˈfər/	
based on	/beɪst ɑn/	

QUESTION TIME

Can you answer these questions?

1 Have you ever cried during a movie?
2 Have you ever spoken to an actor?
3 Have you ever slept in the theater?
4 Have you ever seen a movie more than three times?
5 Have you ever left a movie early?

Study Link MultiROM

CAN YOU REMEMBER...? FILES 8&9

Complete each sentence with one word.

1 A lot of people like rock music. It's ______ popular than classical music.
2 ______ you like to go up in a hot-air balloon?
3 Siberia is the ______ place in the world.
4 Your English is good. You speak very ______.
5 I've never ______ to the US.
6 ______ you ever driven a Ferrari?

How to use your American English File 1 MultiROM

ON YOUR COMPUTER

Grammar Quizzes

There is one Grammar Quiz for each File of the Student Book. Each quiz has 20 questions – each time you do the quiz, the questions appear in a different order.

Study Link Use the Grammar Quizzes to test your grammar after each File of the Student Book. Do the quizzes again later for review. Can you improve your score?

Vocabulary Bank

These exercises review the words and phrases from the Vocabulary Bank pages of the Student Book.

Study Link Use the Vocabulary Bank section of the MultiROM every time you complete a Vocabulary Bank page in the Student Book. Test your memory and improve your pronunciation and spelling.

Sound Bank

The Sound Bank shows you how to pronounce all the vowel and consonant sounds presented in the Student Book. Each sound has five extra example words.

Study Link Use the Sound Bank to help you practice the sounds of English and learn the symbols that represent them in a dictionary. Improve your pronunciation and become a better dictionary user.

Practical English

There is a Practical English section for each Practical English lesson in the Student Book. Each section has two activities – a "Listen and choose" activity and a "Listen and repeat" activity.

Study Link Use Practical English to review and practice the language in the Practical English lessons of the Student Book.

ON YOUR COMPUTER OR CD PLAYER

At the end of each Workbook lesson, there is a Question Time box. Can you answer the questions?

Study Link Use the MultiROM to listen to the questions, repeat them, listen again and answer them. Answer the questions again later for review.

lesson	track
1A	2
1B	3
1C	4
1D	5
2A	6
2B	7
2C	8
2D	9
3A	10
3B	11
3C	12
3D	13
4A	14
4B	15
4C	16
4D	17

lesson	track
5A	18
5B	19
5C	20
5D	21
6A	22
6B	23
6C	24
6D	25
7A	26
7B	27
7C	28
7D	29
8A	30
8B	31
8C	32
8D	33
9A	34
9B	35